GLOBE FEARON
HISTORICAL CASE STUDIES

S0-AJE-210

THE CIVIL RIGHTS MOVEMENT

Teacher's Resource Manual

Globe Fearon Educational Publisher
A Division of Simon & Schuster
Upper Saddle River, New Jersey

Editorial and Marketing Director, Secondary Supplementary: Nancy Surridge
Project Editors: Karen Bernhaut, Ann Clarkson, Lynn Kloss, Carol Schneider
Market Manager, Secondary Supplementary: Rhonda Anderson
Production Director: Kurt Scherwatzky
Production Editor: Alan Dalgleish
Editorial Development: WestEd, Ink
Electronic Page Production: Foca Company
Photo Research: Jenifer Hixson
Interior Design: Foca Company
Cover Design: Joan Jacobus

Grateful acknowledgment is made to the following publishers, authors, and other copyright holders:
Activity Sheet 9: Fred Blackwell, AP/Wide World Photos
Activity Sheet 13: Matt Herron/Black Star

Printed in the United States of America   3 4 5 6 7 8 9 10 00 99 98

ISBN 0-8359-1832-7

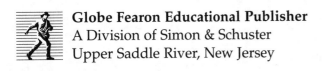

Globe Fearon Educational Publisher
A Division of Simon & Schuster
Upper Saddle River, New Jersey

CONTENTS

HISTORICAL CASE STUDIES: THE CIVIL RIGHTS MOVEMENT

Globe Fearon's *Historical Case Studies: The Civil Rights Movement* offers students a comprehensive look at an event that proved to be a turning point in U.S. history. While many of today's students are keenly interested in the social protest that marked the 1960s and 1970s, they lack an understanding of the intricacies of the history and politics of the United States in relation to protests. In order for them to have meaningful debate about the Civil Rights Movement and its impact on U.S. domestic policy and society, they need deeper background on the movement than conventional texts offer.

The philosophy behind Globe Fearon's Historical Case Studies program is to present a particular event in history in an exciting, yet easy-to-read fashion. The series takes a case-study approach to presenting dramatic human stories that point out the significance of the event for our times. *The Civil Rights Movement* is filled with the drama and color necessary to involve your students in the learning process. Special care has been taken to introduce this complex and sensitive topic in a balanced and straight-forward way.

The book is organized so that material is presented in manageable portions. Each case study focuses on one key event or person related to the Civil Rights Movement. For example, there are case studies on school desegregation in Arkansas, Rosa Parks and the Montgomery bus boycott, Freedom Rides and Freedom Marches, and Malcolm X. An "Overview" chapter introduces the Civil Rights Movement and puts the event into an historical context. A final "Follow-Up" chapter provides perspective on the movement. The profusion of human interest elements gives a *You Are There* quality to the narrative, capturing students' attention for what they are sure to find a fascinating subject.

Historical Case Studies consists of a Student Text and a Teacher's Resource Manual to provide you and your students with the support you need.

The Student Text

The case studies in the Student Text contain the following features to help your students learn the following:

- **Critical Questions** focus students on key issues.

- **Terms to Know** provide students with a list of words and terms used in the case study that might be new to them. Each term on the list is boldfaced and defined when it first appears in the case study. In addition, all words in Terms to Know are included in the glossary in the back of the Student Text.

- **Active Learning** gets students involved in the learning process. Each case study contains an Active Learning project that is introduced at the start of the case study. The projects include conducting an interview, creating posters, and writing an editorial. Throughout each case study there are "hint boxes" reminding students to think about the project and take notes or make sketches about the content they have just read. In the Case Study Review, students are asked to complete their Active Learning project by using the notes or sketches that they made during their reading.

- **Thinking It Over** gives students review questions after each section.

- **Going to the Source** provides a text or visual primary source so that students may hear the words or see the scene through the eyes of someone who was there.
- **Critical Thinking** exercises introduce and reinforce key critical thinking skills.
- **A Good Book to Read** or **A Good Movie to See** suggests a book or video appropriate for students.
- **Case Study Review** poses recall questions, questions on issues for today, and a "What Might You Have Done?" scenario. In addition, there is a cooperative learning project and the conclusion of the Active Learning project at the end of each chapter.

The Teacher's Resource Manual

The Teacher's Resource Manual provides essential support for teaching the case studies. It contains the following elements:

- **Teaching Strategies** give teachers strategies and activities for ESL/LEP students and students with different learning styles. In addition, there are a number of suggested ideas for ongoing activities.
- **Lesson Plans** for each case study, the Overview, and the Follow-Up provide a summary of the case study, a list of content and skill objectives, an activity to open the case study, an activity to develop students' understanding of the case study, an alternative assessment activity, a cooperative learning activity, an activity appropriate for use with ESL/LEP students, an activity to close the case study, guided discussion suggestions for the Lessons for Today and the What Might You Have Done? features in the Student Text, and ideas for projects to extend student understanding.
- **An Annotated Bibliography** contains print and multimedia resources for students and teachers.
- **Reproducible Activity Sheets** reinforce and extend social studies and thinking skills. There are two worksheets for each case study and two each for the Overview and Follow-Up.
- **Tests** offer a one-page exam for each case study, the Overview, and the Follow-Up, to test students' knowledge. Exams will include matching, multiple choice, and essay questions.
- **Answer Key** contains responses to all questions asked in the Student Text, Worksheets, and Tests.

Teaching Strategies For ESL/LEP Students

The ESL/LEP population includes not only students for whom English is a second language, but also native English speakers with limited proficiency. Although the thought of teaching in a language-diverse classroom may seem over-whelming at first, it is comforting to realize that techniques for teaching ESL/LEP students are simply good teaching techniques that are directed toward students' special needs. With an awareness of those needs and what works for students, teachers can easily adapt their instructional styles to language-diverse classrooms.

Strategies

Among effective strategies to consider when developing and presenting lessons for ESL/LEP students are the following:

Modeling: visual or auditory examples for explaining or demonstrating what is expected

Contextual Clues: use of realia, pantomime, gestures, connecting the unknown with the familiar, and acting out meaning when possible

Built-in Redundancy: repetition, para-phrasing, restatement, and use of synonyms

Age Appropriateness: tasks reasonably difficult for the age of the students

Humor: spontaneous and planned humor to reduce anxiety level and increase chances for success

Equal-Status Activities: two-way cooperative interactions between and among learners, such as peer tutoring, inclusion of student interests and experiences, and cross-cultural activities

Cooperative/Collaborative Activities: structured techniques with positive interdependence and individual accountability

Activities and Techniques

Experienced teachers working with ESL/LEP students have some suggestions that may be helpful to first-time teachers of language-diverse students. ESL/LEP teachers recommend that students have a good dictionary. Often, these teachers plan simple questions to get students involved. ESL/LEP teachers provide basic word lists to be learned and memorized for automatic recognition, and they mark the key words in each lesson. The teachers provide an outline of the main ideas and simplify English to increase students' comprehension. ESL/LEP teachers involve students in meaningful interaction. The focus is on meaning rather than on form.

In implementing the ESL/LEP strategies, teachers might consider asking students to do the following additional activities. Some activities might be done in small groups.

- Summarize a paragraph or two, perhaps in your native language. Then, translate your summary into English, using a dictionary.

- Paraphrase a paragraph or primary source (see Going to the Source in every case study).

- Role-play dialogues or events in the history of the Civil Rights Movement with another student who is more proficient in English.

- Make illustrated time lines.

- Create visual displays, such as collages, posters, bulletin board displays, and so forth.

- Write each of the people, places, or events in a particular case study on a series of cards. Then make connections among the cards or arrange them in chronological order.

- Write each sentence of a three- to five-sentence paragraph on separate index cards. Then, arrange sentences in the order that makes the most sense. Explain your answer.

- Relate incidents in the case studies or characters in the case studies to your native language or culture. For example, after you study the civil rights protests, discuss protests in your native country.

- Listen to a taped version of a paragraph, speech, or primary source, and write down unfamiliar words. Explain new vocabulary to another student, replaying the tape as needed.

- Create a "cloze" version of a paragraph—with fill-ins at every fifth word.

- Choose the sentence that explains the main idea of a paragraph and one or two sentences that support the main idea.

- Create picture cards for vocabulary terms.

- Practice tenses by making predictions: for example, How do you think the city government of Montgomery will react to the bus boycotters?

- Play "20 Questions" or "Who Am I?" with other students.

Developing lessons by using the strategies and techniques presented here will help students focus on the essential material in a lesson. Focusing on the essentials enables both teacher and student to work on developing content-area concepts and specific language skills that help students to succeed.

Teaching Strategies For Students with Different Learning and Thinking Styles

People of all ages learn and think in different ways. For example, most people receive information through their five senses, but each individual tends to prefer learning through a particular sense, such as sight or sound. When educators refer to "learning styles," they are basically talking about a unique combination of cognitive, affective, and physiological factors that serve as indicators of how a particular person responds to a learning environment. By keeping in mind the different ways in which students learn and think, teachers can appeal to a range of learning and thinking styles. When different learning and thinking styles are taken into account in planning lessons, teachers can help all their students to understand new information and ideas and to apply this knowledge and insight to their lives.

There are three main learning styles:

■ Visual learners like to see ideas.

■ Auditory learners prefer to hear information.

■ Kinesthetic or tactile learners absorb concepts better when they can move about and use their hands to feel and manipulate objects.

After we receive information, we tend to process or think about the information in one of two ways:

■ Global thinkers prefer to see the "big picture," the whole idea or the general pattern, before they think about the details. They search for relationships among ideas, and they like to make generalizations. They are especially interested in material that relates to their own lives. Global thinkers tend to be impulsive and quick to respond to teachers' questions.

■ Analytical thinkers focus first on the parts and then put them together to form a whole.

They think in a step-by-step approach and look at information in a more impersonal way. They are more likely to analyze information and ideas rather than apply it to their own lives. Analytical thinkers tend to be reflective and thoughtful in their answers.

However, few of us are only auditory learners or only analytical thinkers. Most people use a combination of learning and thinking styles but prefer one modality, or style, over others. An effective lesson takes into account all three types of learning and both types of thinking. The ideas below, in addition to your own creativity, will help you meet the needs and preferences of every student in your class.

Visual Learners

■ Write the Terms to Know on the chalkboard, overhead transparency, or poster so that students can see the words and refer to them.

■ Encourage students to examine the photographs in the case study and to make inferences about the main ideas or topics of the case study.

■ Repeat oral instructions or write them on the chalkboard. After giving instructions, put examples on the board.

■ Use graphic organizers such as word webs, spider graphs, tables, and cause-and-effect charts to help students visualize the information in the case study.

■ Show books in class, or encourage students to watch at home, videos and movies recommended in the student text and on page 44 in this teacher's manual.

Auditory Learners

Invite a volunteer to read aloud the first paragraphs of each case study as students follow along in their books. You might audiotape each case study so that students can listen to it again on their own.

Ask a student to read aloud the Critical Questions at the start of each case study.

Provide time for class and small-group discussions.

Read aloud the directions for each Active Learning feature and for other activities and the questions in each Case Study Review.

Allow students to make oral presentations.

Kinesthetic or Tactile Learners

Encourage students to take notes so that the movement of their hands can help them learn new information.

Encourage students to draw pictures to illustrate content in the case study.

In small groups, ask students to role-play appropriate content in the case study.

Invite students to build or draw models, maps, or memorials when appropriate.

Global Thinkers

■ Explain the "big picture," or the main ideas of the case study first. Point out the Critical Questions at the beginning of each case study.

■ Involve students in brainstorming and discussion groups. Encourage students to express ideas and images suggested by the content of each case study.

■ Explore ways in which the content and information are relevant to students' lives.

■ Encourage students to think about their answers before they respond to questions.

Analytical Thinkers

■ Start with the facts and then offer an overview of the topic in each case study.

■ Give students time to think about their answers before they respond.

■ Whenever possible, help students to create tables for organizing information.

■ Provide time for students to organize concepts in a step-by-step approach.

■ Help students to recognize how the content of the case study relates to their own lives.

Unit Strategies and Ongoing Activities

The lesson plans in the Teacher's Manual for Globe Fearon's *Historical Case Studies: The Civil Rights Movement* offer a number of activities and approaches for teaching each case study. Below are a series of ongoing projects that can be done individually or in groups. You can use these activities to bridge the case studies in the text or to reinforce or extend comprehension of a single case study.

Word-a-Day Calendar

Post a large calendar on the bulletin board. Start or end each class by asking students to record at least three new words that they have learned that day. At regular intervals, such as at the end of a case study or at the end of the week, review these words by playing a game of "pictionary." Assign teams of students to illustrate the words in each of the days or weeks covered on the calendar. Challenge other teams to guess the word. As an extension, ask students to define and spell the word correctly. (Tip: Students can keep their own individual word-a-day-calendars in their notebooks.) This activity is also appropriate for ESL/LEP students.

Class Reference Books

As an ongoing study tool for both ESL/LEP students and for students who are proficient in English, students can design any one of the following three reference books: a biographical dictionary, a gazetteer, or a class dictionary. To help students get started, you might place three-ring notebooks divided by alphabetical tabs at the front of the classroom. At the end of every section or case study, encourage students to develop lists of people, places, or terms that caught their attention. Ask them to write a brief description or definition for each item on a separate sheet of loose-leaf paper. At the end of the entry, students should record the page in the text where each item can be found. Students should then place their entries alphabetically in the appropriate reference book.

Class Time Lines

To help students understand chronology and put events in perspective, ask volunteers to set up time lines for each case study. Ask students to use sheets of butcher paper or connected strips of computer paper to develop wall-sized time lines. Time lines should be divided into appropriate intervals for the unit of study. Also encourage students to leave enough room on their time lines for illustrations or written entries. Select "class historians" on a rotating basis to record entries on the time line on a daily or weekly basis. Periodic review of the time line will help students identify patterns of change, predict trends, and/or spot cause-and-effect relationships.

Peer Teaching

As a cooperative learning activity, you might assign teams of students to teach or review parts of a case study. Suggest that students prepare at least one handout and/or one visual aid. Tell the "teachers" to create a short in-class assignment for students to do. The "teachers" should also write several questions for use in a self-evaluation test at the end of the chapter or unit.

History Log

Whenever you assign a case study, you might ask an individual or group of students to imagine that they are one of the characters in the case study. Ask them to write a series of personal observations about special events or developments mentioned in the case study. Whenever possible, entries should be dated. Then ask volunteers to read their entries aloud. Ask students to guess the identity of the historical person who wrote each set of observations. As an extension, you might distribute the entries for peer editing. Ask students to underline selections of entries that they think are well written. Also encourage them to make corrections or to suggest changes that would improve the writing.

Library Field Trip

Although your students may have been in a library on many occasions, you might want to upgrade their library skills by preparing "field trips" in which students use a variety of reference materials to look up information on select topics in each case study. You can organize a field trip that would be like a scavenger hunt in which students must track down information in a variety of reference sources, such as atlases, encyclopedias, card catalogues, special collections (like record or tape collections), periodical indices, and so forth. For example, if you are studying Case Study 1: Jim Crow Is Expelled from School, you might ask students to collect the following items:

■ A handwritten copy of three to five entries in *The Reader's Guide to Periodical Literature* on the 1954 Supreme Court decision on *Brown v Board of Education of Topeka Kansas* (If possible, students should try to get a photocopy or microfilm printout of one of the articles.)

■ A handwritten copy of a subject or title entry in the card catalogue or computer catalogue on school segregation and desegregation in the 1950s and 1960s

■ A biography of Thurgood Marshall

■ Notes from an encyclopedia entry on Thurgood Marshall or *Brown v Board of Education of Topeka Kansas*

■ A children's book on the Civil Rights Movement with a chapter or section about school desegregation (To obtain such a book, students may have to go to a different section or room in the library.)

After setting up one field trip/scavenger hunt as a model, you might ask volunteers to take turns preparing other field trips. After each field trip, ask students to present their findings and report how they found each item.

Freewriting About History

Periodically, ask students to identify major topics studied in a single case study or block of case studies. Next, tell students to pick one of the topics. Then, set a time limit of three to five minutes and ask students to write nonstop about their topic. (ESL/LEP students can write in their primary language or in a mix of English and non-English.) When students are done, tell them to review their writing to identify important or new ideas on the topic. With the class as a whole, list these ideas in sentence form on the chalkboard. (ESL/LEP students should first translate their sentences into English.) Encourage students to arrange these sentences into paragraphs, adding transition sentences as needed.

THE CIVIL RIGHTS STRUGGLE

Learning Objectives

After completing this case study, students will be able to

■ discuss the impact of *Plessy* v. *Ferguson* (1892) on civil rights for African Americans.

■ describe the conditions under which African Americans lived during the early 1900s.

■ explain the goals and methods of the NAACP.

■ describe the effect of the Great Depression and World War II on African Americans.

Summary

Since the days of slavery, African Americans have struggled to gain equal rights in the United States. After the Civil War and the emancipation of enslaved African Americans, the fight for equal rights increased. Reconstruction brought many gains, but in the years after the antebellum period African Americans again suffered from discrimination.

In 1892, Homer A. Plessy decided to challenge a Louisiana law that segregated African Americans and whites on trains. Plessy argued that separating the races violated the Fourteenth Amendment of the Constitution. His case was heard by the Supreme Court. The Court upheld the Louisiana law, ruling that separation of the races was legal as long as equal facilities were provided. The Court's "separate but equal" decision was a huge step backward for African American civil rights.

Throughout the early 1900s, conditions worsened for African Americans—especially in the South. Jim Crow laws and lynchings made life unbearable. Many African Americans moved to the North in hopes of a better life. They found conditions somewhat better, but far worse than they had hoped to find.

The Great Depression of the 1930s hit African Americans especially hard. However, World War II ended the economic depression and opened jobs in industry and the armed forces to African Americans. After the war, African Americans began to hope for a better future. The Civil Rights Movement began based on that hope. During the 1950s and 1960s, many African Americans and whites decided that it was time to shatter the "color line"—to challenge old laws and make new ones that would bring equality to all U.S. citizens.

Getting Started

Write the term *civil rights* on the chalkboard. Have a volunteer look up the term in the dictionary or in the glossary in the back of their text. Ask students if they can name some of the civil rights to which all U.S. citizens are entitled. You may wish to distribute a copy of the Bill of Rights to help students develop a list of rights. Then, tell students that in the Overview they will read about events that preceded the Civil Rights Movement.

Developing the Lesson

To help students organize and put into context the information presented in the Overview, have them create a chart with two columns. Tell students to label the first column "Event" and the second column "Effect on the African American Community." In the column labeled "Event" direct students to list the following:

■ *Plessy* v. *Ferguson* (1892) is argued before the Supreme Court

a wave of lynchings sweeps the South during the late 1800s

the Great Migration brings thousands of African Americans to the North

the NAACP is formed

The Great Depression hits the U.S. economy

Have students work individually or in groups to use the Overview to find the effect of each one of the events on the African American community.

Alternative Assessment

Drawing a Political Cartoon Have students review the information on Jim Crow laws in their text. Then ask them to create a political cartoon depicting the effect of Jim Crow laws on African Americans in the South. You may wish to show students examples of political cartoons and point out the use of symbols to represent people, countries, and ideas.

Cooperative Learning

Creating Maps and Charts Have groups of students find out more about the Great Migration of African Americans to the North. Ask groups to use library resources to create a chart or a map showing the movement of African Americans to the North. Charts and maps should include the following information:

the years the Great Migration occurred

approximately how many African Americans moved North

from what Southern states or regions did African Americans leave for the North

to which Northern cities did African Americans move

Have groups display their maps and charts in class.

ESL/LEP Strategy

Making an Illustrated Dictionary Have students review the Terms to Know listed at the start of the Overview on page 5. Ask students to use a dictionary or the glossary in the back of their text to find the definition of each word on the list. In addition, have them define other words in the Overview that are new to them. Next, have students create an illustrated dictionary using original drawings or pictures cut from old magazines or newspapers to illustrate as many of the words on the list as possible. Tell students to use a separate sheet of paper for each word. On that sheet of paper, they should write the word and its definition, and paste or tape the picture. Then have them arrange the pages of their dictionary in alphabetical order. You may wish to have students repeat this activity for each Case Study they read.

Closing the Lesson

In closing, ask students to discuss what they think were the key issues faced by the African American community after World War II. Have them brainstorm ways the African American community might have fought discrimination and segregation in education, employment, housing, and other areas in the past.

Extending the Lesson

You may wish to offer the following assignment as extra credit or to enhance students' portfolios.

Creating a Biographical Portrait Have students find out more about W.E.B. Du Bois. Ask them to find out:

■ when and where he was born

■ where he was educated

■ his views on racial equality

■ the role he played in the NAACP

Students may be interested in reading Du Bois's autobiography, which covers his life in the Civil Rights Movement and his travels in Russia and China.

JIM CROW IS EXPELLED FROM SCHOOL

Learning Objectives

After completing this case study, students will be able to

- describe the inequalities that African Americans faced in education in the 1940s and 1950s.

- explain how the Supreme Court reached its verdict in the *Brown* v. *Board of Education* case.

- write an essay about segregated schools. (Active Learning)

- evaluate the validity of "separate but equal" policies. (Critical Thinking)

Summary

In Case Study 1, students learn about the landmark case *Brown* v. *Board of Education, Topeka* (1954). During the 1940s and early 1950s, a number of African Americans in the South decided to take legal action against a segregated education system. In an early case, Levi Pearson and a small group of African American farmers sued the Board of Education in Clarendon County, South Carolina. They tried to win equality in school transportation for their children. However, they lost their case.

The *Brown* case came before the Supreme Court in 1954. Thurgood Marshall headed the team of prosecuting lawyers in the case. Marshall argued that "separate but equal" facilities based on race denied African Americans "equal protection under the law" as guaranteed by the Fourteenth Amendment. The Court found in favor of Brown, bringing new hope to those who sought to end segregation.

Getting Started

Write the phrase "separate but equal" on the chalkboard. Ask students if they are at all familiar with this phrase. Students who have read the Overview in the student text will remember it. Ask them to explain what the phrase means or in what context they have heard it used.

If students are unfamiliar with the phrase, explain that "separate but equal" was a term used to justify segregation between African Americans and whites in the past. You may wish to have students unfamiliar with the term review the Overview on pages 5–10 in the student text.

Developing the Lesson

Ask students to review the information in Section 1, under Standing Up for What Is Right, about Levi Pearson. Ask students to pretend that they are Pearson and that they wish to write a letter to the Board of Education of Clarendon County, South Carolina. In the letter they should request equal bus service for their own children and for other African American children in the county. Remind students that their letters should describe the inequalities between the school bus services that whites and African Americans receive. They should also state exactly what they expect the Board of Education to do about the situation.

After students have written their letters, ask them to imagine that they have received a response from the Board of Education. The Board has denied their requests. Instruct students to write a letter to Thurgood Marshall asking for his assistance in the case against the Board of Education. Ask volunteers to read their letters aloud to the class.

Alternative Assessment

Summarizing Tell students to use the *Reader's Guide to Periodical Literature, The New York Times Index,* and other resources in their local or school library to find articles about the case of *Brown* v. *Board of Education* (1954). If necessary, explain how these indexes work and how students can find periodicals in the library.

Ask students to find at least three articles about the *Brown* case. After they have read the articles, ask each student to write a one- or two-paragraph summary of each article. If possible, ask students to make copies of one or two of the articles that they have found. Post the articles and the summaries on a bulletin board in the classroom or create a scrapbook of the articles and summaries.

Cooperative Learning

Creating a Storybook Divide students into groups of three or four. Ask the groups to review the information about Thurgood Marshall in the case study. Tell the groups that their task is to create a plan for a storybook about Thurgood Marshall for third graders.

Instruct the groups to list the steps involved in creating the storybook. Steps might include:

■ outlining the major events in Marshall's life

■ deciding how long to make the storybook (A length of 6 to 10 pages would be appropriate.)

■ deciding what kinds of pictures to include in the book

■ writing the narrative

Then tell students to divide the tasks in the activity among group members. You may wish to distribute *Activity Sheet 4: Organizing Personal Information* to help students organize information about Marshall's life. Encourage students to find out more about Marshall's life by using resources available in their school or local library.

ESL/LEP Strategy

Developing Vocabulary Ask students to list and define the following words in their notebook.

Tell them to use the glossary in the student text and a dictionary to find the definitions.

■ literacy

■ psychology

■ unanimous

■ investigate

■ inferior

■ discrimination

■ superintendent

■ timber

■ harvest

■ impact

■ chamber

■ doctrine

After they have defined the words, ask students to use each word in a sentence that explains its meaning. Finally, have students write a paragraph summarizing the *Brown* case by using as many of the words on the list as possible.

Closing the Lesson

Review the decision of the Supreme Court in the *Brown* v. *Board of Education* case with students. Tell them that when the Supreme Court made its decision, 40 percent of the children in public schools in the United States attended segregated schools. However, the *Brown* case did not bring about the immediate integration of segregated schools. Ask students: Why did Thurgood Marshall appear before the Supreme Court in 1955—a year after the *Brown* case had been decided? Why do you think the Court's decision in *Brown* v. *Board of Education* failed to bring immediate change to many schools in the Deep South? What does the fact that the Court's decision in *Brown* was ignored by many Southern communities say about segregation and racism?

Extending the Lesson

You may wish to offer the following assignments as extra credit or to enhance students' portfolios.

Writing a Biography Ask interested students to write one- or two-page biographies about one of the following African Americans mentioned in this case study: Jackie Robinson, Paul Robeson, Langston Hughes, or Zora Neale Hurston.

Linking Past to Present Ask students to find out ways in which their federal or state government has been involved in education in recent times. Possible topics include: Bussing during the 1970s and 1980s or movements toward a national curriculum in the 1990s. You may wish to have students find out about federal programs in your community.

Guided Discussion

Lessons for Today (See page 21 in the Student Text.) After students have read the Lessons for Today questions, ask them if they know how public schools are funded. You may need to explain that schools are funded by tax dollars collected from people in the community. In addition, public schools receive money from the state and federal governments. Based on this information, ask students to explain why some schools would have more money than other schools.

Tell students to discuss whether they think the system for school funding is fair or unfair. Ask them to explain why they feel the way they do. Encourage students to think about the criteria that they use to evaluate whether or not something is fair. Ask them if they can think of ways in which the system could be made more equitable.

What Might You Have Done? (See page 21 in the Student Text.) After students have read the scenario, ask them to make a list of the pros and cons of helping Levi Pearson. Ask them to consider how joining Pearson would affect their families, their jobs, and their safety. On the other hand, ask them to consider the benefits of winning equal rights for their children.

After they have finished the task, ask pairs of students to compare their lists. Then tell the pairs to role-play a dialogue between Levi Pearson and a neighbor in which Pearson tries to convince the neighbor to join him in suing the county. Ask volunteers to perform their dialogues for the class.

THE MOB AT CENTRAL HIGH

Learning Objectives

After completing this case study, students will be able to

■ describe the events that took place at Central High School in Little Rock, Arkansas, in 1957.

■ explain why the federal government had to send troops to Little Rock.

■ write a newspaper article about the events that took place at Central High School. (Active Learning)

■ identify and analyze several forms of propaganda in 1957. (Critical Thinking)

Summary

This case study covers the integration of Central High School in Little Rock, Arkansas, in 1957. As a result of the Supreme Court decision in *Brown v. Board of Education of Topeka, Kansas* (1954), schools were ordered to desegregate "with all deliberate speed." Most Southern communities were not eager to integrate African Americans into the white school system. The events that took place at Central High School serve as an example of the extremes that some whites were willing to go to halt desegregation. These same events show the bravery of the nine African American students who were willing to risk their lives in order to make the *Brown* decision become a reality.

Getting Started

Tell students that this case study is about nine African American students who volunteered to attend an all-white high school in the South. Remind them of the Supreme Court's decision in *Brown v. Board of Education* and if necessary refer them to Case Study 1.

Read the following quotation to the class. Tell students that the qoutation is from a radio broadcast on September 4, 1957—the first morning the African Americans were scheduled to attend Central High School.

Hundreds of Little Rock citizens are gathered in front of Central High School awaiting the arrival of the Negro children. We are told people have come from as far away as Mississippi, Louisiana, and Georgia to join forces to halt integration.

Initiate a brief discussion with your class about how the nine students must have felt when they heard this broadcast.

Developing the Lesson

Begin a discussion with students on the importance of analyzing the causes and effects of historical events. Explain that "causes" are events or conditions that lead to a major event or development and that "effects" are events or conditions that happen because of the event. To illustrate the concepts of cause and effect, draw the chart below on the chalkboard, or copy it and distribute it to your class.

Cause ←	Event →	Effect
White mobs turn to violence to prevent the Little Rock Nine from attending Central High	President Eisenhower sends troops to Central High	The Little Rock Nine attend Central High, guarded by federal troops

Divide students into small groups. Ask each group to create a cause-and-effect chart similar to the one above for each of the following *events:*

- White Citizens' Councils are formed throughout the South.
- The Little Rock Nine are barred from entering Central High School on September 4, 1957.
- On September 23, 1957, the Little Rock Nine enter Central High School for the first time.

When students have finished their charts have them draw the charts on the chalkboard. Then, have students explain their choices of causes and effects for each event.

Alternative Assessment

Writing a Diary Entry Ask students to try to remember how they felt on their first day at a new school. Then ask them to review the text describing Elizabeth Eckford's and Melba Pattillo's attempts to enter Central High School for the first time. Ask students to imagine that they are Eckford or Pattillo. Then ask them to write a diary entry for one of the girls, describing what happened and how she felt. Ask students to exchange diary entries with another classmate. Instruct partners to critique one another's work and to offer suggestions on how to improve the diary entries. Then ask students to revise their diaries based on their partner's critiques. Ask volunteers to read their diary entries aloud.

Cooperative Learning

Writing a Scene Divide students into groups of four or five. Tell groups that their task is to write one scene for a movie about the events that took place in Little Rock in 1957–58. Each group should choose one scene from the case study that they wish to portray. If students are having difficulty choosing a scene, present them with the following suggestions:

- Elizabeth Eckford tries to enter the school, gets turned away, and makes her way to the bus stop.
- Governor Faubus makes a speech to a group of his supporters.

- Melba Pattillo's family spends the day together before her first attempt to attend Central High School.
- The Little Rock Nine enter Central High for the first time; and the mob outside of the school goes wild.
- Federal troops escort the African American students to and from classes.
- Jefferson Thomas and Terrence Roberts are attacked by white students.

Tell students that they should first write a paragraph describing the action in the scene that they wish to portray. Then have them list the characters and settings in their scenes. Finally, have students write some sample dialogue for their scenes.

ESL/LEP Strategy

Writing a Letter Review with students the proper format for writing a letter. Tell students that letters to government officials must be properly addressed and organized in order to receive attention. Ask students to review the portion of the case study that deals with the Arkansas governor, Orval Faubus. Remind students that Faubus used the following arguments to justify his racist policies:

- The community of Little Rock is not ready for integration.
- The relationship between the races is good in Little Rock.
- People who want to integrate society are doing it for their own selfish reasons.
- Integration is a Communist idea.

Ask students to restate Faubus's arguments in their own words. Then ask them to brainstorm ways to counter these arguments. Some students may want to list their ideas in their native languages and then translate their ideas into English. Next, ask students to work in pairs to review Faubus's arguments and their own counterarguments. Then ask them to work together to compose a letter to Governor Faubus expressing their thoughts on the subject of integration.

Closing the Lesson

Tell students that a couple of years after the desegregation of Little Rock's schools, some African American students began to boycott stores that discriminated against black customers. Students who supported the boycott wore badges that said: "I am wearing 1959 clothes with 1960 dignity." Ask students what they think that slogan means. Lead them to understand that African Americans were eager to leave behind a segregated past and march into a future in which there was hope for equality.

Extending the Lesson

You may wish to offer the following assignments as extra credit or to enhance students' portfolios.

Writing a Biography Interested students might want to prepare a one- or two-page biography on Daisy Bates. Bates was president of the Arkansas state chapter of the NAACP. She was very involved with the Little Rock Nine. Students could begin their research by reading Bates's book, *The Long Shadow of Little Rock.*

Interviewing Ask students to interview an adult who remembers the events discussed in this case study. Students might ask family members or people from their community for an interview about the events at Little Rock. Tell students to first write down seven to ten questions they wish to ask. Remind them to take detailed notes or, if possible, to record the interview. Finally, ask students to report what they learned about Little Rock from their interview. Some students may wish to invite the person they interviewed to class and conduct a classroom question-and-answer session.

Guided Discussion

Lessons for Today (See page 34 in the Student Text.) After students have read and answered the questions in the Lessons for Today section, you may wish to discuss the issue of going against the group with your students. Begin the discussion by asking students the following questions: Why is it difficult to go against the group? What is your opinion of a person who goes against the group? Do you respect that person more or less? Why?

Some students in your class may be willing to share their own experiences or discuss the experiences of a friend who acted independently. If so, have them explain why they or their friend were able to go against the group. Ask them to explain why it was difficult for them to act independently and how they felt about their decisions.

What Might You Have Done? (See page 34 in the Student Text.) Before students begin this assignment, ask them to think about the criteria that guides them when they offer advice to someone. Ask: What do you consider most important when you offer your advice or your opinion to another person? If students are having difficulty determining their criteria, ask some leading questions. For example, ask them: Do you consider the age of the person to whom you are giving advice? Does it make a difference whether the person is a friend, an adult, or a family member?

When they have completed the assignment, encourage students to discuss the advice they offered President Eisenhower. Find out whether any of your students offered a course of action different from that which the President actually took at Little Rock.

ROSA PARKS AND THE MONTGOMERY BUS BOYCOTT

Learning Objectives

After completing this case study, students will be able to

- explain the significance of the Montgomery bus boycott in the Civil Rights Movement.
- describe the reasons for the boycott's success.
- work with classmates to write a skit about the Montgomery bus boycott. (Active Learning)
- understand the value of evaluating points of view when deciding on an individual course of action. (Critical Thinking)

Summary

Case Study 3 tells the story of Rosa Parks and the Montgomery bus boycott. Students will read about Parks's refusal to relinquish her seat on the bus to white passengers. Parks's subsequent arrest led to a boycott that many mark as the start of the Civil Rights Movement.

The Montgomery bus boycott lasted more than a year. The boycott did more than win desegregation of city buses. It brought such leaders as Martin Luther King, Jr., to the forefront of African Americans' struggle for civil rights. The boycott also demonstrated the power of nonviolent protest. Nonviolent protest would be the hallmark of the first phase of the Civil Rights Movement.

Getting Started

Tell students that Case Study 3 covers the Montgomery bus boycott. It is likely that a number of your students will be familiar with the names Rosa Parks and Martin Luther King, Jr. Ask students what they know about the role these two people played in the struggle for African American civil rights.

Then read the following quote to your students. Explain that the quote is the impression of a 13-year-old African American boy who participated in the boycott.

> *When the boycott started, I just couldn't wait for morning to come because I wanted to see what was happening. I walked to school. As the buses passed me and my schoolmates, we said, "Nobody's on the bus! Nobody's on the bus!" It was just a beautiful thing. It was a day to behold to see nobody on the bus.*

Initiate a brief discussion with your class about how this boy felt and why.

Developing the Lesson

To help students understand the sequence of events in the Montgomery bus boycott, list the following statements on the chalkboard or copy and distribute them to the class. (For your reference, the number in parentheses after each statement indicates the chronological sequence in which the event took place.)

- The Supreme Court rules on the case brought by the bus boycotters. (11)
- Parks is found guilty of violating Montgomery's segregation laws. (3)
- E. D. Nixon brings up the idea of a one-day boycott to the African American community of Montgomery. (5)
- Rosa Parks refuses to give up her seat on a Montgomery city bus. (2)
- African American churches and boycott leaders' houses are bombed. (9)

The Montgomery Improvement Association is formed to lead the boycott. (6)

E. D. Nixon and Jo Ann Robinson organize a meeting at the Dexter Avenue Baptist Church. (4)

Rosa Parks loses her job. (7)

Montgomery's buses are desegregated. (12)

Rosa Parks, Martin Luther King, Jr., and about 80 other boycotters are arrested for conspiring "to conduct an illegal boycott." (8)

Martin Luther King, Jr., becomes minister at the Dexter Avenue Baptist Church. (1)

Boycotters file a suit charging that Montgomery's system of segregated buses is illegal. (10)

Ask students to work individually or in small groups to put the statements in order. Then have students create an illustrated time line of the events. They may wish to add more events concerning the boycott to their time lines. Students might also add world events to their time lines as well.

Alternative Assessment

Creating a Leaflet Ask students to imagine that they have volunteered to help write and distribute leaflets telling the African American community of Montgomery about the planned bus boycott. Ask them to write a leaflet informing people of the boycott and explaining why it is important to take part in it.

You may wish to read the following excerpt from the leaflet that was distributed to your students:

> [A] Negro woman has been arrested and thrown in jail because she refused to get up out of her seat on the bus for a white person to sit down. . . . This has to be stopped. Negroes have rights too, for if Negroes did not ride the buses, they could not operate. Three-fourths of the riders are Negroes, yet we are arrested, or have to stand over empty seats. . . . We are, therefore, asking every Negro to stay off the buses Monday in protest of the arrest and trial. Don't ride the buses to work, to town, to school, or anywhere on Monday.

Assign Activity Sheet 7: Interpreting a Leaflet to help students analyze the contents of the leaflet.

Cooperative Learning

Interviewing Divide students into groups of four or five. Tell them that their assignment is to organize a talk show featuring leaders and participants of the Montgomery bus boycott. As their first step, the group should decide who they would like to interview. Possibilities include Rosa Parks, E. D. Nixon, Jo Ann Robinson, and Martin Luther King, Jr. Students may want to include on their talk show an African American citizen who participated in the boycott. Encourage students to use library resources to find out more about the boycott and those who took part.

After students have decided who will be on their show, ask them to formulate questions to ask the guests. Have them devise possible answers to their questions. Next, ask students to decide which member of their group will play the host of the show and who will play each guest. Then, tell groups to rehearse their show. After you have given them time to prepare, have each group perform its show in class.

ESL/LEP Strategy

Formulating Questions Tell students to create and play a *Jeopardy*-like game. To become familiar with the content presented in this case study, explain that in the game of *Jeopardy*, an answer to a question is given. Players must provide the question for the answer. Therefore, it is important to remember to respond in the form of a question. Use the examples below to practice the format of the game with your students.

1. A: He was an Indian leader who inspired Dr. Martin Luther King, Jr.'s, use of nonviolence in the fight for civil rights.
   Q: Who was Gandhi?

2. A: Rosa Parks refused to give up her seat on a bus in this city.
   Q: What is Montgomery?

3. A: It is Martin Luther King, Jr.'s, birthplace.
  Q: What is Atlanta, Georgia?

After students understand the format of the game, tell them to work in pairs to write three to five Jeopardy questions and answers. Collect students' work and use the best examples to quiz the class.

Closing the Lesson

Remind students how bus boycotters responded when they were asked about the boycott. One older woman said, "I'm not walking for myself. I'm walking for my children and my grandchildren." When asked if she was tired, another walker said, "My feet are tired, but my soul is rested."

Ask students to think about what the boycott meant to these people and the others who refused to ride the buses during the boycott. Ask them how they might have responded to a reporter's questions if they had participated in the boycott.

Extending the Lesson

You may wish to offer the following assignments as extra credit or to enhance students' portfolios.

Researching Jo Ann Robinson was a teacher at Alabama State College, then an all–African American institution. She was head of the Women's Political Council, a group of African American, professional women. Ask students to find out more about Robinson or about the role of women in the Montgomery bus boycott. Ask them to present their findings to the class in the form of an oral report.

Linking Past to Present Ask students to find out about the effectiveness of more recent boycotts. For example, students may wish to research the boycott that some companies staged against South Africa during the era of apartheid.

Guided Discussion

Lessons for Today (See page 47 in the Student Text.) After students have read the questions, you might try a brainstorming session to help students come up with reasons why people participate in boycotts. Write the word "boycott" on the chalkboard. Ask students to list words they associate with boycott. Then ask students the first question: "What concerns did leaders of the boycott have after the first day?" If students are still having trouble answering the question, refer them to the case study. Tell students to work in small groups to answer the rest of the questions.

What Might You Have Done? (See page 47 in the Student Text.) Before students write their responses to the question, ask them if they think they would encourage their friends to seek revenge on the bomber or to seek a peaceful way to fight the bomber. Ask them to explain their responses.

SITTING IN FOR JUSTICE

Learning Objectives

After completing this case study, students will be able to

- describe the impact of the lunch counter sit-ins on the Civil Rights Movement.

- explain how the Student Nonviolent Coordinating Committee (SNCC) was founded.

- create storyboards accompanied by narration for a documentary on the sit-in movement. (Active Learning)

- evaluate moral responsibility for segregation. (Critical Thinking)

Summary

In 1960, four African American college students from the South decided to take action against segregation between African Americans and whites. They decided to try to integrate the lunch counter at the F. W. Woolworth store in Greensboro, North Carolina. The students used a form of protest that became known as a "sit-in."

The actions of the four students sparked a nationwide movement against segregation in public places. African Americans and a number of whites began waves of protesting in the South and in the North.

The lunch counter sit-ins that took place over the next several years led to the desegregation of lunch counters and stores all over the South. But the impact of the sit-ins went beyond the integration of lunch counters. The sit-ins inspired African Americans to demand integration of other public facilities such as parks, pools, and churches. The sits-ins also led to the founding of the Student Nonviolent Coordinating Committee (SNCC). SNCC became a leading organization in the struggle for civil rights.

Getting Started

Read aloud the opening paragraphs before Section 1 on page 50 of the Student Text to your class. Explain to your students that everyone, at some point in life, feels like an outcast. Ask students to think about a time when they felt out of place. On the chalkboard, write the following:

I felt awkward when _____.

Give students a minute or two to complete the sentence. Encourage them to write another sentence or two to elaborate their ideas on the situation. Be sure students understand that they do not have to share their responses with the class.

When they have finished, ask them to imagine feeling or being treated like an outcast all the time. Tell them that in Case Study 4 they will read about a group of young people who decided that they no longer wanted to feel that way.

Developing the Lesson

Ask students to imagine the following situation:

It is the early 1960s. You are an African American living in the South. You and a friend have decided to integrate a lunch counter in a department store. You've walked into the store and purchased a few items. Then you sit at the lunch counter and wait for service.

Now write the following dialogue on the chalkboard or copy and distribute it to your class.

White Waitress: What are you doing up here? You know you can't eat here.

You: Why can't I? I shop here and you take my money for that. Now I'd like to order lunch, please.

White Waitress: You have to go. You can't eat up here. You know better.

You: _____

After students have finished reading, tell them to complete the dialogue by explaining how they and their friend might respond to the waitress. Ask students to imagine that they have been trained to use nonviolent tactics. Further, ask them to imagine that the manager comes over and threatens to call the police.

Tell students to work in pairs to write the dialogue. Then have pairs volunteer to read their work aloud.

Alternative Assessment

Writing a Song Tell students that three young women who served time in a Florida jail for participating in a sit-in at a Woolworth's lunch counter wrote a song called "Fight On." Read students the following lyrics from the song:

> _Gone to the jail, without paying our bail_
> _Justice will come right over the trail. . . ._
> _We're fighting, we're fighting, for a better_
>   _land we know._
> _For the Consititution tells us so_
> _Fight on, fight on._

Ask students to write one or two more verses to "Fight On" or to compose an original song or poem about the sit-ins.

Cooperative Learning

Making a Map Divide students into small groups. Tell the groups that their assignment is to create a map showing the locations of the sit-ins described in the case study. First, tell students to use an atlas or a textbook to find a map of the United States that shows state borders and cities. Next, instruct them to trace a map of the Eastern portion of the United States. Tell them to trace the state borders. Then ask students to review the case study and list the cities in which sit-ins took place. You may wish to have students use classroom or library resources to find additional locations.

Tell students to mark the locations of the sit-ins on their maps. Encourage groups to create a

symbol to note the locations of the sit-ins and to create a map key for the symbol. Finally, tell groups to devise an appropriate title for their maps.

You may wish to have groups keep their maps to note the locations of other protests and events during the Civil Rights Movement.

ESL/LEP Strategy

Creating Headlines Tell students to work in pairs to create two sets of newspaper headlines for the events covered in this case study. You may wish to bring a newspaper into class and ask students to study headlines for form and content.

Tell students that for their first set of headlines they should imagine that they work for a newspaper in the North. Their job is to write headlines for articles about the sit-ins. Have them write three to five headlines describing the events.

After they have completed the task, tell them to imagine that they work for a newspaper in the South. Their task is the same, except that they must write headlines for articles that might have appeared in a newspaper in the South.

Discuss the differences in the two sets of headlines. Then display the students' headlines on a bulletin board in the classroom.

Closing the Lesson

In closing, ask students to discuss the following question: Why do you think young people were so active in the Civil Rights Movement?

After discussing the question, read the quotation below to students. Tell them that the quotation contains the words of Gladys Williams, an African American high school student from Montgomery who took part in the sit-ins.

> _Going to jail, oh, it was a badge of honor during_
> _that time! When you demonstrated, you already_
> _knew it's possible you're going to jail. It's pos-_
> _sible you're gonna get hurt. It's possible you're_
> _gonna get killed. But our minds were made up._
> _We had an understanding with the Lord that_
> _this was what we wanted to do. And He was_

always out there with us. So as far as having fear, we didn't even know what fear was. We just had our minds set on freedom, and that was it.

Ask students: Why was Williams willing to risk jail and beatings to participate in sit-ins and other demonstrations?

Extending the Lesson

You may wish to offer the following assignments as extra credit or to enhance students' portfolios.

Drawing Posters Ask students to create posters that ask students at a college in the South to join a sit-in. Ask students to decide in which city and in which store they intend to hold their sit-in. Tell them to think of images and words for the poster that might convince students that it is important to be a part of the sit-in.

Researching Ask interested students to find out more about the other protests that the sit-ins inspired, such as the wade-ins, read-ins, and kneel-ins. Tell students to report their findings to the class.

Guided Discussion

Lessons for Today (See page 59 in the Student Text.) After students have read the questions, ask them to note the use of the words *"good or moral"* in the questions. Tell students to consider the criteria they apply when deciding whether something is *"good or moral."* Tell students to work in small groups to discuss their criteria. Then ask each group to share its ideas with the class. It is more than likely that different students have different criteria for making their decisions. Ask students how the differences among people's ideas complicates the issues they are asked to think about in this question.

As a follow-up tell students to complete the Critical Thinking Exercise: Examining Moral Responsibility for Segregation on page 59.

What Might You Have Done? (See page 59 in the Student Text.) You may wish to ask small groups of students to role-play the scenario suggested in the questions. Ask students to work together to write a brief skit portraying a conversation between Blair and his parents.

FREEDOM RIDES AND FREEDOM MARCHES

Learning Objectives

After completing this case study, students will be able to

- describe how racist Southerners responded to the Freedom Rides of 1961.
- discuss the outcomes of the marches in Birmingham and Washington, D.C., in 1963.
- conduct interviews about the Freedom Rides and Freedom Marches. (Active Learning)
- defend their opinions on civil rights. (Critical Thinking)

Summary

In Case Study 5, students will learn about the Freedom Rides of 1961, the 1963 march in Birmingham, and the March on Washington. Throughout the Civil Rights Movement, protesters put themselves into danger to further the cause of racial equality. Perhaps the most dangerous type of protest was the Freedom Ride. Freedom Riders sought to test the South's compliance to a law banning segregation on interstate buses. Riders rode interstate buses into the South where they were frequently beaten and jailed. In the end, however, the federal government pressured Southern communities into ending segregation on buses and in other public places.

Dr. Martin Luther King, Jr., led the marches that took place in Birmingham, Alabama, in 1963. Like the Freedom Riders, King and the civil rights protesters used nonviolent tactics to fight racism. Their opponents used violence and jailings to try to stop the protesters. Despite the violence, the civil rights marchers persisted. They succeeded in bringing an end to segregation in Birmingham.

Civil rights leaders staged a march on Washington in August 1963 as a way of pressuring Congress into passing pending civil rights legislation. The march was a huge success, culminating in the now-famous "I Have a Dream" speech by Martin Luther King, Jr. The following year, Congress passed and President Lyndon Johnson signed the Civil Rights Act of 1964.

Getting Started

Tell students to read aloud the story about James Farmer and Bayard Rustin that opens this case study. Then tell students that Farmer decided to stage the Freedom Rides of 1961 because he believed, "We put on pressure and create a crisis" for government leaders "and then they react." Ask students to respond to Farmer's statement before they begin reading.

Developing the Lesson

Ask students to create a chart to organize the information in this chapter. Tell them to draw a chart in their notebooks with three columns and four rows. Next, tell them to label the columns "Freedom Rides," "March in Birmingham," and "March on Washington." Tell them to label the rows "Date," "Goal," "How goal was achieved," and "What impressed me most about this protest was..." See the chart below.

Ask students to work individually or in pairs to complete their charts. After students have finished, review their answers and discuss their impressions of the events discussed in the chapter.

	Freedom Rides	March in Birmingham	March on Washington
Date			
Goal			
How goal was achieved			
What impressed me most . . .			

Alternative Assessment

Writing an Article Ask students to write an article or a series of articles on one of the following topics:

- Attacks on Freedom Riders in the South
- Martin Luther King, Jr.'s, arrest in Birmingham on April 12, 1963
- Teenagers join the marches in Birmingham
- March on Washington in 1963

Encourage students to draw or describe pictures to accompany their articles. Ask student volunteers to collect the articles and create a classroom "special edition" newspaper on the Freedom Rides and Freedom Marches.

Cooperative Learning

Writing a Speech Tell students to review Section 3 of the case study on the March on Washington. Divide students into groups and ask them to imagine that they have been asked to address the crowd in Washington. Tell them to write a speech, a poem, or a song, that they might deliver at the march.

First, ask students to decide what message they want to convey to the crowd. Tell them to outline their message with examples and details. Next, ask them to write a first draft of their speech. After they have reviewed their drafts, tell them to revise it. Tell each group to choose one member to read the speech. Tell that member to practice giving the speech in front of his or her

group. Other group members should give advice on how to improve the presentation of the speech. Finally, tell each group to present its speech to the class.

ESL/LEP Strategy

Designing a Monument Tell students to imagine that it is the year 2011 and they have been chosen to design bus stop monuments to commemorate the 50th anniversary of the Freedom Rides. Tell students to work in small groups to decide what type of monument to build. Ask them to figure out what form they want their monument to take. Remind them that monuments can be created as sculptures, plaques, statues, or other forms. You may wish to point out to them various monuments in your city or town.

First, tell students to sketch a picture of their monuments. Then, ask them to create three-dimensional mini-models of their designs. You may wish to supply them with clay, papier-mâché, or other materials.

Closing the Lesson

Share with students the following story about the Freedom Riders. As students have read, President Kennedy sent federal marshals to help the Freedom Riders and other people trapped inside the church in Montgomery. After doing so, he asked civil rights leaders for a "cooling off" period. To that request James Farmer replied, "We had been cooling off for 100 years. If we got any cooler, we'd be in a deep freeze." Ask students to discuss the federal government's response to the Freedom Riders and the marches in Birmingham and Washington.

Extending the Lesson

You may wish to offer the following assignments as extra credit or to enhance students' portfolios.

Analyzing a Speech Ask students to find an audio or text version of Martin Luther King, Jr.'s, "I Have a Dream" speech. After they have listened to and/or read the speech, ask them to answer the following questions:

1. What promise did King say the Constitution and the Declaration of Independence make to U.S. citizens?

2. What did King mean when he warned African Americans not to "seek to satisfy our thirst for freedom by drinking from the cup of bitterness and hatred"?

3. What does King say about white people?

4. Summarize the dream of Martin Luther King, Jr.

Preparing a Biographical Profile Ask students to find out more about one of the following leaders of the Civil Rights Movement.

■ James Farmer, founder of the Congress on Racial Equality (CORE) and leader of the 1961 Freedom Rides

■ Bayard Rustin, one-time nightclub entertainer turned civil rights organizer and aide to A. Philip Randolph

■ John Lewis, chairman of the Student Nonviolent Coordinating Committee (SNCC) and Freedom Rider

■ Roy Wilkens, a leader in the NAACP

■ Ralph Abernathy, a minister, close associate, and aide to Martin Luther King, Jr.

Ask them to find out what role these leaders played in the Freedom Rides and/or the March on Washington. Have students present their findings to the class in an oral report.

Guided Discussion

Lessons for Today (See page 72 in the Student Text.) After students have read the questions, ask them to think of situations in which the United States has intervened in the affairs of other countries. Have the class work together to list some examples of U.S. intervention. Then conduct a discussion about whether the United States was protecting its own interests or the interests of the other country or both.

After this discussion, have students apply the same reasoning to answer the questions presented in Lessons for Today.

What Might You Have Done? (See page 72 in the Student Text.) Ask students to work individually or in groups to write their speeches. Ask them to first outline their thoughts before they write their speeches. Encourage volunteers to read their speeches before the class.

FREEDOM SUMMER, 1964

Learning Objectives

After completing this case study, students will be able to

■ discuss the goals and methods used by volunteers during Freedom Summer 1964.

■ describe the causes and effects of riots in African American communities in the North during the summer of 1964.

■ create posters for a television special on Freedom Summer. (Active Learning)

■ read critically to determine author bias. (Critical Thinking)

Summary

In Case Study 6, students will read about Freedom Summer, 1964. Freedom Summer was the effort by civil rights workers to hold a summer-long voter registration drive for African Americans in Mississippi.

The state of Mississippi had long been a place where African Americans were treated badly, even by the standards of the Deep South. Voter registration among African Americans in the state was the lowest in the country. It was a place where civil rights workers did not expect to be welcomed by the white authorities.

Freedom Summer brought together volunteers from the North and South to reach out to the African American community in rural Mississippi. The volunteers sought to register people to vote and to set up Freedom Schools to teach adults and children subjects ranging from math to foreign languages.

The summer was marked by moments of triumph and moments of deep sorrow. There were murders, bombings, and threats. There were also moments of hope and triumph. The formation of

the Mississippi Freedom Democratic Party (MFDP) was one such moment. The party offered an integrated alternative to the all-white regular Democratic party in Mississippi. Led by people such as Fannie Lou Hamer, the group attempted to replace the segregated party at the 1964 Democratic Convention.

In this case study, students will also learn about the effects of racism in the North and the riots that occurred in ghettos across the nation during the summer of 1964.

Getting Started

Tell students that when President Lyndon Johnson signed the Civil Rights Act of 1964 in July, he said that the act made "those who are equal before God now equal in the polling booths, in the classrooms, in the factories, and in hotels and restaurants and movie theaters and other places that provide service to the public." Explain to your students that just a year before Johnson signed the Civil Rights Act, a white man in Baker County, Georgia, said, "It doesn't make any difference what Congress and the Supreme Court *say* the law is. It won't matter here *this* generation!" Lead students in a discussion in which they contrast these two quotations. Then tell them that in this case study they will read about the events that were part of the Civil Rights Movement in the summer of 1964.

Developing the Lesson

After students have read the case study, divide them into small groups. Tell them that their task is to compare the conditions of African Americans in the North to those in the South. Draw a Venn diagram on the chalkboard. (See below.) Tell students to copy and fill in the diagram on

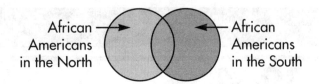

African Americans in the North

African Americans in the South

a large sheet of paper. Show the students how to fill in the different sections of the diagram. The overlapping area in the center is for similarities between the two groups, while the outside areas are for the differences.

After students have completed their diagrams, ask them to answer the following questions:

1. What differences existed between the conditions of African Americans living in the South and North?

2. What similarities were there?

3. Why do you think riots took place in African American communities in the North and not in the South?

4. Why did President Johnson declare a "War on Poverty"?

Alternative Assessment

Writing a Letter Ask students to imagine that they are Northerners who have volunteered to take part in Freedom Summer. Ask them to read the excerpt from the article featured in Going to the Source on page 80 in their Student Texts.

Tell students to freewrite their *immediate* impressions of the charges described in the article. Then ask them to respond to the article with a letter to the editor of the newspaper. Remind them to challenge the following points in their letters:

■ It is unbelievable that a thousand college students would come to the South to participate in voter registration drives on their own.

■ The students have been taken advantage of by Communists and left-wingers.

■ The parades publicizing the disappearance of Chaney, Schwerner, and Goodman were organized long ago, implying that their disappearance was staged.

■ The ultimate aim of Freedom Summer is a black revolution, a race revolution, and the destruction of the U.S. government.

Cooperative Learning

Analyzing a Document Divide students into groups of three or four. Ask them to imagine that they have volunteered to teach at a Freedom School. Tell them that the students have requested a lesson on the Bill of Rights. Ask students to locate a copy of the Bill of Rights. You may be able to find an annotated copy in a U.S. history textbook.

Explain to your students that the Bill of Rights is the first ten amendments to the Constitution. These amendments, added to the Constitution in 1791, serve as legal protection of individual rights in the United States. Ask students to read the amendments and to summarize each one in a sentence or two. Then ask each group to create a poster that they could use to teach the Bill of Rights at a Freedom School. Ask students: Which of the amendments do you think were most relevant to African Americans during the Civil Rights Movement? Encourage students to explain their answers.

ESL/LEP Strategy

Understanding Cause and Effect Ask students to list the goals of the Freedom Summer project on a sheet of paper or list the following goals on the chalkboard:

■ Start Freedom Schools for African Americans who were denied an education.

■ Help educate African Americans who lived in rural areas.

■ Work to increase voter registration.

■ Build a new political party that would be open to all races.

Review any vocabulary that may be unfamiliar to students. Such words might include: denied, rural, and political party. After students understand the goals, explain that an "effect" is the result of an action. Ask students to list at least one effect of each of the goals of Freedom

Summer. Then, ask volunteers to write the effects on the chalkboard. Discuss the importance of Freedom Summer with your students and ask them which of the goals they think was the most important and why.

Closing the Lesson

In closing, reread what Fannie Lou Hamer said when asked whether she was afraid to fight for her rights. "What was the point of being scared?" she said. "The only thing they could do to me was kill me. It seemed like they'd been trying to do that a little bit at a time ever since I could remember." Ask students to discuss reasons that Hamer would make this statement and the qualities she possessed that gave her the courage to fight for her rights.

Extending the Lesson

You may wish to offer the following assignments as extra credit or to enhance students' portfolios.

Conducting a Mock Trial Ask interested students to form a group and to do more research into the murders of Chaney, Goodman, and Schwerner. Ask students to conduct a mock reenactment of the trial of the men accused of murdering the three civil rights workers.

Writing a Biography Ask students to use library and classroom resources to research Fannie Lou Hamer's life. Ask them to create an eight- to ten-page illustrated book about Hamer for elementary-age schoolchildren.

Guided Discussion

Lessons for Today (See page 86 in the Student Text.) After students have read the questions, ask them to explain why it is important to vote. Then, tell them to work in small groups to formulate a plan for increasing voter registration. First, ask them to identify various age groups and cultural groups that have low voter registration. Next, ask them to identify possible causes for low voter turn-out in each group. Finally, ask them to choose one of the groups to target in their campaign.

What Might You Have Done? (See page 86 in the Student Text.) It may be helpful for students answering this question to work in pairs to brainstorm a list of pros and cons associated with helping Hamer in registering African Americans to vote. Then ask the pairs to create a dialogue between Hamer and the farmer. After they have rehearsed their dialogues, encourage students to perform them for the class.

THE BITTER STRUGGLE OF MALCOLM X

Learning Objectives

After completing this case study, students will be able to

- explain how and why Malcolm X joined the Nation of Islam and the effect it had on his life.
- describe the effect Malcolm X had on the Civil Rights Movement.
- write several diary entries from a particular point of view. (Active Learning)
- compare different points of view. (Critical Thinking)

Summary

In Case Study 7, students will read about Malcolm X, one of the most controversial figures in the history of the Civil Rights Movement. Born Malcolm Little, he was influenced by his father's activism and leadership in the Marcus Garvey Universal Negro Improvement Association (UNIA). Garvey preached that people of African descent from around the world needed to recapture an inner strength and independence as a people.

As a youngster, Malcolm Little was an excellent student and was popular with white as well as African American classmates. After the death of his father, the Little family was torn apart. Little's mother became ill and Malcolm and his young brothers and sisters were sent to foster homes.

During the time when he lived with his sister in Boston, Little turned to a life of crime. He was arrested in 1946 for theft. It was during his time in prison that he changed his life. While in prison, Malcolm Little learned about the Nation of Islam and became a member. He dropped the name Little and adopted the letter X to symbolize his lost African name.

As a member and representative of the Nation of Islam, Malcolm X preached the group's message of strict separation of blacks and whites. A dynamic speaker, Malcolm X recruited many African Americans to the Nation. He quickly rose to a position of authority, but soon after came into conflict with the leader of the organization. He left the group in 1964.

Malcolm X then traveled to the Middle East and Africa. The trip proved to be another turning point in his life. After the trip, Malcolm changed his mind about all whites being bad. He decided that it was U.S. society that was racist and that African Americans should work to win political power. But Malcolm X's vision was cut short when an assassin's bullet cut him down in 1965.

Getting Started

Before students begin this case study, read them the quotation below. It is from a speech Malcolm X made in October 1963.

> *America is faced with her worst domestic crisis since the Civil War. The worst crisis since the Revolutionary War. For America now faces a race war. The entire country is on the verge of erupting into racial violence and bloodshed simply because 20 million ex-slaves here in America are demanding freedom, justice, and equality from their former slavemasters.*

Initiate a brief discussion with your students on what Malcolm X is saying in this quote. Ask students to compare this message to that of Martin Luther King, Jr.

Developing the Lesson

Ask students to write an editorial in which they give their opinions of Malcolm X's contributions to the Civil Rights Movement. Begin by telling students that an editorial is a feature in a newspaper in which the writer gives his or her opinion about something with supporting facts. You might bring several examples of editorials to class to illustrate style and content.

Tell students to review the case study and choose an event in Malcolm's life or to consider his whole life. Then ask them to freewrite for three minutes explaining how they feel about the events of Malcolm X's life. Tell students to review their freewriting and choose sentences and phrases that best explain their opinions. Next, ask students to shape those sentences and phrases into complete thoughts and to write a first draft of their editorial. Have students work with a partner to critique their first drafts and to suggest revisions. Finally, ask students to revise their editorials. Encourage volunteers to read their finished editorials aloud.

Alternative Assessment

Writing a Scene Ask students to work individually or in groups to write a scene for a play or a movie based on one of the episodes in Malcolm X's career described in the case study. If students are having difficulty thinking of ideas for scenes, you may share the following list with them:

■ The Little family's house in Lansing, Michigan is burned down.

■ Malcolm Little tells his teacher that he wants to be a lawyer.

■ Malcolm Little is sent to jail for burglary and becomes a Muslim.

■ Malcolm X and Martin Luther King, Jr., meet and discuss their views.

Tell students to write a description of the action in their scenes. Next tell them to decide which characters their scene will include. Then ask them to write a draft of the dialogue. After they have revised their first draft, ask students who are working in groups to read their dialogues to the class.

Cooperative Learning

Creating a Newspaper Ask students to work in groups to create a newspaper about Malcolm X's role in the Civil Rights Movement. Tell groups to first brainstorm a list of topics on which they would like to write articles. To help students get started, you may wish to provide them with the following list of possible topics:

■ Malcolm X converts to Islam.

■ Malcolm X preaches to thousands, winning converts to the Nation of Islam.

■ What life was like in Harlem or other black ghettos during the 1950s and 1960s.

■ Malcolm X's travels abroad change his outlook.

Tell students that they should have each member of their group write at least one article for the paper. Encourage students to use school and library resources to write their articles. Tell students that before they write the final drafts of their articles, they should have an "editorial meeting" to decide how they want to lay out their paper. Also, ask them to think of a title for their newspaper. Tell them to make a list of illustrations or photographs to accompany their articles. They may leave space for pictures and insert either photocopies of pictures, drawings or sketches of pictures, or descriptions of pictures. Finally, tell students to print or type their articles and lay them out on a large sheet of butcher paper or poster paper. If you have access to a desktop publishing program, you may wish to lay out articles on the computer. Display the completed newpapers in class.

ESL/LEP Strategy

Using Active Verbs Tell students that in speaking or writing one may use an active or passive voice. Active verbs are stronger and more direct than the passive form of verbs. Write the following example on the chalkboard:

Passive: The conversion of Malcolm X to the religion of Islam changed his life.

Active: Malcolm X's conversion to Islam changed his life.

Then write the following passive sentences on the chalkboard or copy and distribute them to the class. Ask students to change the sentences from passive to active. The answers appear in italics after each sentence.

■ The founder of the Universal Negro Improvement Association was Marcus Garvey. (*Marcus Garvey founded the Universal Negro Improvement Association.*)

■ The Little family's house was burned to the ground by racists. (*Racists burned the Little family's house to the ground.*)

■ It was while he was in jail, that Malcolm converted to Islam. (*Malcolm converted to Islam while in jail.*)

■ The philosophy of Elijah Muhammad was that whites were evil. (*Elijah Muhammad believed that whites were evil.*)

■ The message that Malcolm X preached was one of unity and progress. (*Malcolm preached a message of unity and progress.*)

Closing the Lesson

Read the following quotation to your students. It is a quotation by Alex Haley, who helped Malcolm X write his autobiography shortly before Malcolm X's assassination.

> *When I first came to know Malcolm, my perceptions were that most white people . . . ranged from being very, very apprehensive about Malcolm to hating Malcolm. . . . That was not too far afield of probably the majority of black people also. Nowadays you might hear a lot of people talking about how they followed him and so forth, but my perception at that time was that the large majority were frightened by the things Malcolm said. . . . But there were those who were empathetic with the Nation of Islam, or were feeling that Malcolm was having the courage to say aloud, publicly, things which they had felt or which they wished somebody would say. So the blacks' reaction was a mixed one, from some who were terrified by what he was saying to those who cheered and applauded when his name was mentioned, let alone when he came into sight.*

Ask students how Haley explains African Americans' reaction to Malcolm X. Why do you think some were afraid of him? Why do you think some cheered him? Ask students their opinion of Malcolm X now that they have read this case study.

Extending the Lesson

You may wish to offer the following assignments as extra credit or to enhance students' portfolios.

Analyzing a Quotation Marcus Garvey made the statement below in 1928. Distribute the quotation to students and tell them to rewrite it in their own words.

> *No race has the last word on culture and on civilization. You do not know what the black man is capable of; you do not know what he is thinking and therefore you do not know what the oppressed and suppressed Negro, by virtue of his condition and circumstance, may give to the world as a surprise.*

Linking Past to Present Ask interested students to find out about the Nation of Islam today. Ask them to report their findings to the class.

Guided Discussion

Lessons for Today (See page 100 in the Student Text.) After students have read the questions, write the word *martyr* on the chalkboard. Lead students toward defining the word as "a person who makes great sacrifices in order to further a belief, cause, or principle." Then, ask students whether they would call Malcolm X a martyr. Encourage them to explain their opinion. Then tell students to work in small groups to discuss and formulate answers to the questions in the text.

What Might You Have Done? (See page 100 in the Student Text.)

To answer the question in this section, you may want students to work in pairs to role-play the scenario. Tell one student in each pair to pretend to be Malcolm and tell the other to pretend to be the friend. Ask pairs to volunteer to perform their role plays for the class after they have had time to prepare.

BLACK POWER!

Learning Objectives

After completing this case study, students will be able to

■ identify the roots of the Black Power movement and discuss its place in the history of the Civil Rights Movement.

■ describe the riots that shook cities in the North from 1965 to 1967.

■ write a skit on the meaning of Black Power. (Active Learning)

■ compare and contrast the ideas of the Black Power movement with those of the old leadership of SNCC. (Critical Thinking)

Summary

The Civil Rights Movement changed in tone and direction during the mid to late 1960s. New leaders such as Stokely Carmichael demanded an immediate end to racial discrimination. The new leadership rallied under the banner of Black Power. They advocated separation from white society rather than integration.

In the beginning of the Civil Rights Movement, the focus was on changing conditions for African Americans in the South. The South was seen as a stronghold of racism and discrimination. By the mid-1960s, protests by African Americans in the North became louder. Although African Americans in the North were not subject to Jim Crow laws, they still faced discrimination. Barred from the best jobs, schools, and housing, generation after generation of African Americans found themselves caught in a cycle of economic depression, drugs, and violence.

During the mid-1960s, African Americans' patience broke with a stronger call for a break in the cycle of poverty and violence. Riots rocked ghettos in major cities such as Los Angeles, Newark, Detroit, and Chicago. Groups such as the Black Panthers formed and advocated the use of militant methods to achieve their goals. By 1967 the U.S. government published a study on race relations in the United States. The Kerner Commission characterized the country as a nation divided by race. The violence in the cities and the report of the Kerner Commission forced the United States to take a serious look at the way African Americans were treated.

Getting Started

Ask students to scan the photographs, captions, section titles, and subsection headings in this case study. Based on their observations, ask them to formulate two or three questions that they think will be answered by reading the case study. Tell students to record their questions in their notebooks or on a large sheet of paper in the classroom. As they read Case Study 8, ask students to refer to their questions and answer those that they can.

Developing the Lesson

Tell students to imagine that they have the opportunity to interview one of the people mentioned in the chapter about the rise of the Black Power movement. Tell students to work in pairs and to decide whom they wish to interview. Possible subjects are

■ James Meredith

■ Martin Luther King, Jr.

■ Stokely Carmichael

■ Fannie Lou Hamer

■ John Lewis

Huey Newton

Bobby Seale

Otto Kerner (head of the Kerner Commission)

Encourage students to use library resources to find out more about their subjects.

Tell pairs of students to create a list of questions that they wish to ask the person whom they will interview. Then tell students to draft answers that they think their subjects might be likely to give. After each pair of students has prepared their questions and answers, encourage volunteers to conduct their interviews for the class.

Alternative Assessment

Creating a Poster Ask students to create posters to gain support for one of the following:

the Black Power movement

the Black Panthers

a black studies program at a school

Tell students to think of words and images that they could use on the posters. Display finished posters in the classroom.

Cooperative Learning

Debating Organize students into teams to debate the following issue: In which direction should the Civil Rights Movement have gone in the mid-1960s? One team will argue that the Civil Rights Movement should have continued to follow Martin Luther King, Jr., and the integrationists. The other team will argue that the movement needed a new direction and that Stokely Carmichael's idea of separation was a better choice.

Tell each team to use the Student Text and library resources to build support for their arguments. Tell students to carefully consider the other team's point of view and to think of evidence to counter it.

Begin the debate by giving each team several minutes to make an opening statement. Then tell teams to begin stating their positions and refuting one another. End the debate by allowing each team several minutes to make closing remarks.

ESL/LEP Strategy

Making a Concept Map Discuss using a concept map as a means of organizing ideas. Explain that it consists of connected circles that help to visually link main ideas and supporting details.

Ask students to decide what is the main topic of Case Study 8. Write it on the chalkboard and draw a large circle around it. Now ask what

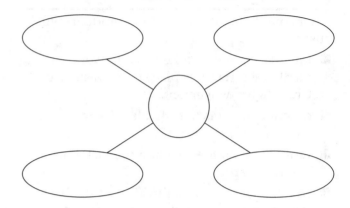

main ideas were part of this topic. When two or more main ideas are decided on by the class, put those ideas in circles on either side of the topic. Finally, look for details that support each of the main ideas. Record these supporting details and connect them to the appropriate circles in the concept map.

Closing the Lesson

Bring to class, or ask students to bring to class, recent newspaper and magazine articles about inner-city life today. Tell students to summarize one or two articles and discuss their content in class. Ask them to comment on aspects of inner-city life that they think seem to have changed since the 1960s. Ask them what they think seems to have remained the same.

Extending the Lesson

You may wish to offer the following assignments as extra credit or to enhance students' portfolios.

Researching Ask interested students to research the history of the Student Nonviolent Coordinating Committee (SNCC). Tell them to share with the class what they have learned in an oral report.

Writing a Newspaper Article Ask students to write a newspaper article describing how James Meredith was shot and how the march from Memphis to Jackson, Mississippi proceeded. Remind students to include the split between Martin Luther King, Jr.'s method of protest and that of Stokely Charmichael.

Guided Discussion

Lessons for Today (See page 113 in the Student Text.) After students have read the questions, ask them to brainstorm a list of things that they would like changed in their school or their community. For each item on the list, ask them to describe the problem or condition as it is now and how they would like to see it changed. Then encourage students to work in small groups to develop their plans.

What Might You Have Done? (See page 113 in the Student Text.) After students have read the question, tell them to list the pros and cons of both the old-timers and the young hawks. Then tell students to work in small groups to role play a conversation among three people: a supporter of Stokely Carmichael, a supporter of John Lewis, and a person who is undecided.

THE ROAD PARTLY TRAVELED

Learning Objectives

After completing this case study, students will be able to

- list and describe the major accomplishments of the Civil Rights Movement.
- discuss the findings of the Kerner Commission.
- formulate questions for an interview. (Active Learning)

Summary

In the Follow-Up, students learn about the Civil Rights Movement during the late 1960s. In 1967 and 1968, Martin Luther King, Jr., began a fight against poverty. Dr. King believed that poverty was the United States's main enemy. He was planning a march on Washington in April 1968. However, on April 4 King was assassinated. His death signaled the end of an era. The movement for civil rights would never be the same.

The Civil Rights Movement had accomplished a great deal. More African Americans than ever were voting. Schools and public facilities were integrated. The movement also stood as an example for other groups facing discrimination, to fight for their rights. Still, much remains to be done to ensure that the United States provides equal justice and opportunities for all its citizens.

Getting Started

Ask students to list the accomplishments of the Civil Rights Movement and to describe how these accomplishments have helped the African American community at large. Then have students brainstorm problems that the African American community faces today. Tell students

to think about ways these problems can be addressed using the methods of the Civil Rights Movement or other methods.

Developing the Lesson

Ask students to work individually or in small groups to create a time line of major events in the Civil Rights Movement. Have students use a large sheet of paper or pieces of computer paper taped together to draw their time lines. Tell them that their time lines should begin in the year 1945 and should end in 1970.

As an extension of this activity, you might have students add other events in U.S. history and world history to their time lines. Tell students to list at least 15 events from the Civil Rights Movement and 15 U.S. and world events.

Alternative Assessment

Writing a Letter Have students compose letters to their representatives in Congress or their local politicians explaining the need for a monument to Civil Rights Workers in their state or town. Ask students to think about the kind of monument they would suggest and where it should be placed.

Cooperative Learning

Creating a Museum Catalogue Tell your class that their task will be to plan a museum exhibit on the Civil Rights Movement and to produce a catalogue for their exhibit. To make sure that students understand the task, you might ask students if they have recently been to a museum and have them describe the exhibit they saw. Alternatively, you might plan a visit to a local museum or library that is having an art or artifact exhibition. Also, bring museum catalogues for students to browse through.

Divide students into groups of three or four. Have each group brainstorm a list of ideas for an exhibit on the Civil Rights Movement. Next, have groups read their list aloud and write each item on the chalkboard. Try to get between 10 and 15 items on the list. If there are too many, you may wish to eliminate some by holding a class vote.

Assign each group two to three items from the list to research. Have them decide exactly what it is they would show, how they would display it, and how they would describe it in a catalogue. Then have groups write a description of their items and sketch pictures or use photos from old newspapers and magazines to illustrate the item. Finally, have each group use one sheet of paper for each item on their list. On the sheet of paper, combine the illustration of an item and its description. Then organize the sheets of paper into a binder. If possible, make multiple copies of the catalogue for students to take home.

ESL/LEP Strategy

Making a Word Web Have students use the term "civil rights" to create a word web of categories from The Civil Rights Movement. Categories might include: Martin Luther King, Jr., Sit-ins, Kerner Commission, etc. Then have each student choose one category and continue the word web. Finally, help students write a paragraph explaining the connection between the category, person, or event in their word web and the Civil Rights Movement.

Closing the Lesson

Read the following quote by President John Kennedy to students: "In giving rights to others which belong to them, we give rights to ourselves and to our country." Ask students to discuss the meaning of the quote and to talk about its relation to the Civil Rights Movement.

Extending the Lesson

You may wish to offer the following assignment as extra credit or to enhance students' portfolios.

Researching the Vietnam War Have interested students find out about the role of African Americans in the Vietnam War. Ask students to find out how many African American soldiers fought in the war and what percentage of the total armed forces they made up. Then have students find out about the discrimination African Americans faced in the armed forces. Have them present their findings to the class.

Guided Discussion

Lesson for Today (See page 122 in the Student Text.) After students have read the question, organize them into small groups to discuss their feelings about the issue. Have the groups assign one person to record the groups' attitudes. Finally, ask groups to share their opinions with the class.

What Might You Have Done? (See page 122 in the Student Text.) You may wish to have students do the activity listed under Extending the Lesson. With information they have gathered they can write their speech for the civil rights activists.

The Civil Rights Movement: A Bibliography

Print Material

Books preceded by an (s) are recommended for students. The recommendations are based on the readability and "student friendliness" of the book, but you are the best judge of your students' abilities and should only consider these recommendations as general guidelines.

General

(s) Durham, Michael S. *Powerful Days: The Civil Rights Photography of Charles Moore.* New York: Stewart, Tabori and Chang, 1991. Powerful, disturbing, and graphic photographs cover key events in the Civil Rights Movement from 1955 to 1965, including the Montgomery bus boycott and the Selma march.

Hampton, Henry, and Steven Fayer (eds.). *Voices of Freedom: An Oral History of the Civil Rights Movement from the 1950s through the 1980s.* New York: Bantam Books, 1990. One of several companion books to the PBS series *Eyes on the Prize,* this book is the result of nearly a thousand interviews. It allows the story of the movement to be told by the people who were part of it.

(s) Harris, Janet, *The Long Freedom Road,* New York: McGraw-Hill, 1967. The story of the Civil Rights Movement to 1967. This book provides a brief history of African Americans from the Civil War to the 1950s. It also includes chapters on *Brown* v. *Board of Education,* the Montgomery boycott, the sit-in movement, the March on Washington, the Mississippi Freedom Summer, and the beginning of the movement in the North.

(s) Haskins, James. *One More River to Cross.* New York: Scholastic, 1992. This book presents brief biographies of 12 African Americans who courageously fought against racism to become leaders in their fields. It includes biographies of Fannie Lou Hamer and Malcolm X.

(s) Hine, Darlene Clark, and Clayborne Carson (eds.). *Milestones in Black American History.* New York: Chelsea House, 1995. This book is a 16-volume exploration of the black experience from ancient Egypt to the present. Each book in the series focuses on a specific period of African American history. Several books in the series focus on the various phases of the Civil Rights Movement.

(s) Levine, Ellen. *Freedom's Children: Young Civil Rights Activists Tell Their Own Stories.* New York: G.P. Putnams' Sons, 1993. This book contains the stories of 30 African Americans who were children and teenagers during the civil rights era. Divided into chronological segments, the book's subjects describe their experiences in their own words.

Lowery, Charles D., and John F. Marszalek (eds.). *The Encyclopedia of African-American Civil Rights: From Emancipation to the Present.* Westport, CT: Greenwood Press, 1992. This book provides an accurate and convenient overview of the century-long struggle for civil rights told through more than 100 short articles.

Morris, Aldon. *Origins of the Civil Rights Movement: Black Communities Organizing for Change.* New York: Free Press, 1984. This book traces the roots of the Civil Rights Movement from the 1953 bus boycott in Baton Rouge, Louisiana, to 1963. It explores the connection between local African American churches and the civil rights workers.

(s) Powledge, Fred. *We Shall Overcome: Heroes of the Civil Rights Movement.* New York: Charles Scribner's Sons, 1993. This book tells the stories of ordinary people who took part in the Civil Rights Movement. The focus is on high school and college students who had seen their parents suffer under segregation and who vowed to put an end to it. Participants in the marches, freedom summers, and voter registration movements tell their own stories.

(s) Rochelle, Belinda. *Witnesses to Freedom: Young People Who Fought for Civil Rights.* New York: Lodestar Books, 1993. Describes the experiences of young African Americans who were involved in significant events in the Civil Rights Movement, including *Brown v. Board of Education*, the Montgomery bus boycott, and the sit-in movement.

(s) Sitkoff, Harvard. *The Struggle for Black Equality: 1954–1992.* New York: Hill and Wang, 1993. This book is a highly readable account of the Civil Rights movement from *Brown v. Board of Education* to the 1990s.

(s) Sterling, Dorothy. *Tear Down the Walls! A History of the American Civil Rights Movement.* New York: Doubleday, 1968. This book, which went to press just before the assassination of Martin Luther King, Jr., provides a survey of African American civil rights from the time when the first slave ships arrived to 1968.

(s) Sterne, Emma Gelders. *I Have a Dream.* New York: Alfred A. Knopf, 1965. Each of the ten chapters in this book focuses on a hero in the struggle for civil rights for African Americans. It includes chapters on Rosa Parks, Daisy Bates, James Farmer, and John Lewis.

Case Study 1
Jim Crow is Expelled from School

(s) Fireside, Harvey, and Sarah Betsy Fuller. *Brown v. Board of Education: Equal Schooling for All.* Hillside, NJ: Enslow Publishers, 1994. This book examines the ideas and arguments of the people behind the landmark case.

(s) Hess, Debra. *Thurgood Marshall: The Fight for Equal Justice.* Englewood Cliffs, NJ: Silver Burdett Press, 1990. This book is an accessible biography of Thurgood Marshall, a leader in the Civil Rights Movement. It describes his life from his birth to 1990.

(s) Latham, Frank Brown. *The Rise and Fall of Jim Crow, 1865–1964.* New York: Franklin Watts, 1969. This book discusses the events and court decisions that led to Jim Crow laws which denied African Americans equal treatment. It outlines events and decisions that abolished these laws in the 1960s.

(s) Stevens, Leonard A. *Equal!: The Case of Integration vs. Jim Crow.* New York: Coward, McCann & Geoghegan, 1976. This book traces the history of Jim Crow laws and the most important court decisions concerning them from 1896 to 1976.

Whitman, Mark (ed.). *Removing a Badge of Slavery: The Record of Brown v. Board of Education.* Princeton, NJ: Markus Wiener, 1993. This book presents the record of the landmark case through excerpts from the trial. Introductory material and annotations precede the excerpts, helping readers put the testimony and briefs into perspective.

Case Study 2
The Mob at Central High School

(s) Beals, Melba Pattillo. *Warriors Don't Cry: A Searing Memoir of the Battle to Integrate Little Rock's Central High.* New York: Pocket Books, 1994. One of the Little Rock Nine tells the story of how she and the others survived a year of trauma.

Blossom, Virgil T. *It Has Happened Here.* New York: Harper & Bros., 1959. The superintendent of schools in Little Rock reveals how a law-abiding U.S. city, straining to solve a complex problem, was demoralized by the actions of a few power-hungry men.

Huckaby, Elizabeth. *Crisis at Central High: Little Rock 1957–58.* Baton Rouge, LA: Louisiana State

University Press, 1980. Vice-principal Elizabeth Huckaby tells the gripping story of integration at Central High School.

Case Study 3
Rosa Parks and the Montgomery Bus Boycott

(s) Haskins, James. *The Life and Death of Martin Luther King, Jr.* New York: Lothrop, Lee & Shepard, 1977. Haskins descibes a man who dedicated his life to the cause of civil rights. He also reexamines unanswered questions concerning Dr. King's assassination.

(s) Hull, Mary. *Rosa Parks.* New York: Chelsea House, 1994. This book contains an account of Rosa Parks's life and what inspired her to act on that December day in 1955.

(s) Parks, Rosa, and Jim Haskins. *Rosa Parks: My Story.* New York: Dial Books, 1992. Rosa Parks tells her own story in this autobiography. Written in her own straightforward and moving language, Parks reveals the reasoning behind the choices that she made.

Robinson, Jo Ann Gibson. *The Montgomery Bus Boycott and the Women Who Started It: The Memoir of Jo Ann Gibson Robinson.* Knoxville: University of Tennessee Press, 1987. Robinson explores the role of the Women's Political Council and her own memories of the success of the Montgomery Bus Boycott.

(s) Siegal, Beatrice. *The Year They Walked: Rosa Parks and the Montgomery Bus Boycott.* New York: Four Winds Press, 1992. This book examines the life of Rosa Parks, focusing on her role in the Montgomery bus boycott.

Case Study 4
Sitting In for Justice

Carson, Clayborne. *In Struggle: SNCC and the Black Awakening of the 1960s.* Cambridge, MA: Harvard University Press, 1981. This book explores the development and the demise of the Student Nonviolent Coordinating Committee from the 1950s through the 1970s.

Chafe, William Henry. *Civilities and Civil Rights: Greensboro, North Carolina, and the Black Struggle for Freedom.* New York: Oxford University Press, 1980. This book tells the story of the sit-in movement that began in Greensboro, North Carolina.

Case Study 5
Freedom Rides and Freedom Marches

(s) Cohen, Tom. *Three Who Dared.* New York: Doubleday, 1969. This book describes the activities of three young men who risked their lives to participate in the Freedom Marches and the Civil Rights Movement.

Farmer, James. *Lay Bare the Heart: An Autobiography of the Civil Rights Movement.* New York: Arbor House, 1985. In his autobiography, Farmer describes the conflicts, rivalries, and betrayals within the Civil Rights Movement. He also discusses his encounters with Washington politicians and presidents during the struggle.

Farmer, James. *Freedom—When?* New York: Random House, 1965. As leader of the Civil Rights Movement, Farmer describes two decades of involvement in the quest for equality.

(s) Haskins, James. *The Freedom Rides: Journey for Justice.* New York: Hyperion Books for Children, 1995. This book explains how the Freedom Rides came to be, and why they were so important to the civil rights struggle.

Meier, August, and Elliott Rudwick. *CORE: A Study in the Civil Rights Movement, 1942–1968.* New York: Oxford University Press, 1973. A comprehensive history of the Congress on Racial Equality. Discusses its origins, development, successes, failures.

Case Study 6
Freedom Summer, 1964

Dittmer, John. *Local People: The Struggle for Civil Rights in Mississippi.* Chicago: University of Illinois Press, 1994. This book tells in depth the grim story of the Civil Rights Movement in Mississippi.

Mills, Kay. *This Little Light of Mine: The Life of Fannie Lou Hamer.* New York: Dutton, 1993. This book is a biography examining the life of a remarkable woman.

Payne, Charles M. *I've Got the Light of Freedom: The Organizing Tradition and the Mississippi Freedom Struggle.* Berkeley: University of California, 1995. This book is a groundbreaking history of the early Civil Rights Movement in the South. It describes how early leaders built a strong local network of support that could not be broken despite violence and repression.

(s) Rubel, David. *Fannie Lou Hamer: From Sharecropping to Politics.* Englewood Cliffs, NJ: Silver Burdett Press, 1990. This book follows the life of one of the first African American organizers of voter registration drives in Mississippi.

(s) Walter, Mildred Pitts. *Mississippi Challenge.* NY: Bradbury Press, 1992. The first part of this book describes African Americans in Mississippi from before the Civil War through Reconstruction. The second part discusses the 1960s, describing the impact of the Student Nonviolent Coordinating Committee, the Mississippi Freedom Democrat Party, and the events of Freedom Summer.

Case Study 7
The Bitter Struggle of Malcolm X

(s) Barr, Roger. *Malcolm X.* San Diego, CA: Lucent Books, 1994. This book describes the life of the controversial Black Muslim leader. It emphasizes his philosophies, goals, and legacy.

(s) Brown, Kevin. *Malcolm X: His Life and Legacy.* Brookfield, CT: Millbrook Press, 1995. This book is a biography that explores the life of Malcolm X within several contexts—religion, racism, and the Civil Rights Movement.

Clark, Steve (ed.). *February, 1965, the Final Speeches of Malcolm X.* New York: Pathfinder, 1992. This book is a collection of speeches and interviews by Malcolm X from the last three weeks of his life.

X, Malcolm. *The Autobiography of Malcolm X.* New York: Grove Press, 1965. This book is a riveting autobiography written in conjunction with Alex Haley. It traces the life of Malcolm X from his childhood to his conversion to Islam and his break with the Nation of Islam.

(s) X, Malcolm. *Malcolm X Talks to Young People: Speeches in the U.S., Britain, and Africa.* New York: Pathfinder, 1991. This book features five talks that Malcolm X gave to teenagers in the last year of his life.

Case Study 8
Black Power!

Hilliard, David, and Lewis Cole. *This Side of Glory: The Autobiography of David Hilliard and the Story of the Black Panther Party.* Boston: Little, Brown, 1993. This book is the autobiography of an activist in the black power movement.

Pearson, Hugh. *The Shadow of the Panther: Huey Newton and the Price of Black Power in America.* Reading, MA: Addison-Wesley, 1994. This book tells the story of Huey Newton and the Black Panthers.

Stokely, Carmichael, and Charles V. Hamilton. *Black Power: The Politics of Liberation in America.* New York: Random House, 1967. The authors of this book describe their ideas of black power and how it has and can be used. Organized around themes, the authors explain why they believe that African Americans must define themselves and their own roles and adopt their own methods for liberation through unconciliatory tactics.

Van Deburg, William L. *New Day in Babylon: The Black Power Movement and American Culture, 1965–1975.* Chicago: University of Chicago Press, 1992. This book is an examination of the Black Power Movement within the context of American culture.

Multimedia

Video

Eyes on the Prize, Part I. Alexandria, VA: PBS Video, 1987. Produced by Blackside, Inc. (60 minutes each) The videos are a comprehensive documentary and multiple-award winning series on the Civil Rights Movement. Part I is divided into the six segments listed below.

- Awakenings (1954–1956)
- Fighting Back (1957–1962)
- Ain't Scared of Your Jails (1960–1961)
- Mississippi: Is This America? (1962–1964)
- No Easy Walk (1962–1966)
- Bridge to Freedom (1965)

Eyes on the Prize, Part II. Alexandria, VA: PBS Video, 1990. Produced by Blackside, Inc. (60 minutes each) These videos are a comprehensive documentary and multiple-award winning series on the Civil Rights Movement. Part II is divided into the eight segments listed below.

- The Time Has Come (1964–1965)
- Two Societies (1965–1968)
- The Promised Land (1967–1968)
- Power! (1966–1968)
- Ain't Gonna Shuffle No More (1964–1972)
- A Nation of Law? (1968–1971)
- The Keys to the Kingdom (1974–1980)
- Back to the Movement (1979–mid-1980s)

King: Montgomery to Memphis. Chicago: Films, Inc., 1970. Produced by Kaplan Landau and Martin Luther King, Jr., Foundation. This film is an inspiring look at King's career from the Montgomery bus boycott to his assassination. It includes excerpts from his speeches and interviews with civil rights leaders and members of his family.

Malcolm X: El Hajj Malik El Shabazz. Xenon Home Video, 1991. (60 minutes) This film traces Malcolm X's incredible odyssey from a Harlem street hustler and self-edifying prison inmate to a militant Muslim convert and self-made world leader.

Malcolm X: His Own Story as It Really Happened. Burbank, CA: Warner Home Video, 1972. (92 minutes) This film is adaptation of the autobiography Malcolm X wrote with Alex Haley's assistance.

My Past Is My Own. Santa Monica, CA: Pyramid Films and Video, 1989. (47 minutes) In this film two contemporary African American teenagers are "transported" back to the days of the Civil Rights Movement, where they encounter a segregated world fiercely divided by racial tensions. Whoopi Goldberg plays the role of aunt to the two teens.

The Road to Brown. San Francisco: Resolution, Inc., 1990. (47 minutes) This film provides a concise history of the role Charles Hamilton Houston, a brilliant civil rights attorney, played in the struggle for legal equality for African Americans in the schools.

Section Questions and Chapter Reviews

Overview

Thinking It Over: 1. *Plessy* v. *Ferguson* established the principle of "separate but equal." This allowed whites to legally set up separate facilities for whites and African Americans, which were rarely equal. **2.** The Great Migration was a movement that began in the early 1900s. Large numbers of Southern African Americans migrated to cities in the North in hopes of finding a better life, free of racism.

Case Study 1

Section 1: Thinking It Over: 1. African American schools were run down with little or no facilities. Some schools had no water fountains or running water. None of the African American schools had indoor toilets. Clarendon County spent an average of $43 per year to educate each African American student and an average of $179 on each white student. **2.** They faced the danger of losing their jobs and the possibility of violent attacks by white racists.

Going to the Source: 1. Clark presented two dolls to African American children, one brown and one pink. He asked them to point to the doll that they would prefer to play with. He also asked the children which doll was bad and which one they thought was nice. **2.** Clark concluded that segregation had a harmful and destabilizing impact on African American children.

Section 2: Thinking It Over: 1. Reverend Brown wanted his daughter to attend a local school and to receive an equal education to that of the white students. **2.** Professor Kenneth Clark was a psychologist who testified on the impact of segregation on the mental development of African American students. Clark testified that his work showed that segregation made African American students regard themselves as inferior.

Section 3: Thinking It Over: 1. The Supreme Court ruled unanimously that segregated schools were unequal. **2.(a)** *Brown II* ordered school districts to desegregate "with all deliberate speed." **(b)** African Americans were worried by this decision because it was too vague. It provided no support for immediate action to integrate schools.

Case Study Review *Identifying Main Ideas:* **1.** Levi Pearson sued the school system of Clarendon County in order to win school transportation for African American students that was equal to the transportation available to white students. **2.** Brown sued the Topeka school district to get his daughter into an all-white school that was closer to their home and had better facilities. **3.** The *Brown II* ruling was too vague. Since the ruling didn't specify when schools needed to desegregate, many districts failed to integrate.

Case Study 2

Section 1: Thinking It Over: 1. The White Citizens' Councils strongly opposed the proposed integration and threatened violence to maintain segregation. **2.** Answers will vary, but should suggest that Faubus was referring to people who supported integration. He was trying to weaken the support for integration by linking it with a discredited idea such as communism.

Going to the Source: 1. Eckford's first thought was to make it to safety by walking down the block to the front entrance of the school. **2.** Eckford started getting nervous because the crowd started following her and calling her names.

Section 2: Thinking It Over: 1. The National Guard troops made no attempt to protect the African American students and prevented the nine from entering the school. They were directed by Governor Faubus to keep the students out. **2.** Answers will vary, but the questions should relate in some way to Melba's feelings as she confronted racism at Central High.

Section 3: Thinking It Over: 1. Eisenhower was forced to send federal troops into Little Rock to protect the African American students and force the integration of Central High. **2.** Answers will vary, but could cover the increasing role of the federal government, the power of public opinion, or the fact that the federal troops were integrated.

Case Study Review *Identifying Main Ideas:* **1.** The Arkansas National Guardsmen refused to help the African American students because they were acting under orders from Governor Faubus not to allow the African American students to enter the school. **2.** Daisy Bates was threatened with violence because she worked to organize the nine African American students and to help them enter Central High School. **3.** The violence died down after Federal troops took over the school. However, after things calmed down, control inside the school was returned to the Arkansas National Guard. White students inside the school realized that they were again free to threaten and harass the African American students.

Case Study 3

Going to the Source: 1. One example may be that African Americans had to get on the front of the bus to pay then get off to go to the back to be seated. Often, the drivers would then leave before they reached the back of the bus. **2.** Some answers may include: the bus was crowded, she didn't see the need of getting on the bus twice, or she felt she had the right to enter at the front of the bus.

Section 1: Thinking It Over: 1. Robinson proposed that E.D. Nixon join a boycott that her group was planning. The boycott was of Montgomery's buses to protest the arrest of

Rosa Parks. 2. He warned her that she might be killed by the authorities if she protested her arrest.

Section 2: Thinking It Over: 1. The Kings hesitated because it would subject them and their children to Southern segregation. **2.** Martin Luther King, Jr., believed in nonviolence. He was influenced by the ideas of Mohandas Gandhi.

Section 3: Thinking It Over: 1. Volunteers printed leaflets calling for the boycott and spread them out to the African American community. **2.** Although the first day had been a success, they weren't sure that the boycott would continue successfully. There was pressure to end it while it was still a success.

Section 4: Thinking It Over: 1. The Montgomery Bus Boycott ended when the Supreme Court ruled that Montgomery's bus segregation laws were unconstitutional. **2.** The boycott was successful. Segregation on buses in the city of Montgomery was ended by the boycott.

Case Study Review *Identifying Main Ideas:* **1.** The leaders of the boycott were concerned that the momentum of the first day might not be maintained and the boycott would fizzle. Some counseled protesters to end the boycott, fearing that people would not be able to maintain the sacrifice. **2.** As the boycott got stronger, the boycotters increased their demands to include a call for full equality on the buses. **3.** Reaction was diverse. Some whites supported the boycott. Others threatened African Americans with the loss of their jobs if they did not ride the bus. Other African Americans were threatened with violence or attacked.

Case Study 4

Section 1: Thinking It Over: 1. The Greensboro students were opposing segregation by sitting at the all-white lunch counter. **2.** Blair and his friends were inspired by the Little Rock Nine and by the Montgomery Bus Boycott.

Section 2: Thinking It Over: 1. SNCC was a group of students who organized to coordinate sit-in efforts across the country. **2.** Answers will vary. Some students may point out examples from this chapter and the successes that resulted from non-violent protest.

Going to the Source: 1. The picture shows food and drinks being dumped on the protesters. **2.** Answers will vary. Students may describe the outrage felt by many when they saw this picture.

Section 3: Thinking It Over: 1. "Civil disobedience" is an act of breaking a law that a person thinks is unjust. The leaders of the sit-ins used civil disobedience, an idea learned from Martin Luther King, Jr., and Gandhi as a protest tactic. **2.** Answers will vary. Students might point out examples in history where this tactic has been successful.

Section 4: Thinking It Over: 1. John Lewis was the son of a sharecropper family who led the early Nashville, Tennessee, sit-ins. Julian Bond was a student in Atlanta who led sit-in efforts there. **2.** The businessman meant that it took the pressure of the sit-ins, and the impact on local businesses to make the white business community ready to accept integration.

Case Study Review *Identifying Main Ideas:* **1.** African Americans and whites from neighboring states heard about the Greensboro sit-in and used it to fight their own state's segregation laws. **2.** After the formation of SNCC, the sit-in movement was better organized. Demonstrators were trained by SNCC on how to conduct a sit-in and how to protect themselves. **3.(a)** Marshall's faith for change was in the courts and feared that sit-ins would become violent. **(b)** The NAACP provided legal support for protesters who had been put in jail.

Case Study 5

Section 1: Thinking It Over: 1. The Freedom Rider bus was attacked outside of Anniston, Alabama. The bus was fire bombed, and the Riders were beaten as they emerged from the bus. **2.** Connor refused to prevent an angry mob from beating Freedom Riders by claiming that his troops had the day off in observation of Mother's Day.

Section 2: Thinking It Over: 1. The Birmingham civil rights leaders allowed students to march in the protests because the demonstrations were weakening since so many adults had been arrested. **2.** The persistence of the demonstrations, the concern of business leaders about the decline in business, and bad publicity toward the city were all responsible for the decision to grant the demands of the protesters.

Going to the Source: 1. Answers will vary. Students might note that the Declaration of Independence was a protest document that was created in opposition to unjust laws under the British government. **2.** Whether all Americans are entitled to equal rights and equal opportunity under the law.

Section 3: Thinking It Over: 1. The March on Washington was sparked by the murder of Medgar Evers. The march was also organized to rally enough public support to force approval of President Kennedy's Civil Rights Act. **2.** Lyndon Johnson signed the Civil Rights Act. President Kennedy had been assassinated in November 1963.

Case Study Review *Identifying Main Ideas:* **1.** Answers will vary. Some students may answer, Freedom Riders helped integrate interstate buses, and expose the brutality of racism in the South. **2.** Martin Luther King, Jr., chose Birmingham as the focus of his campaign because Birmingham was a large and prosperous city with a large African American population that did not share in the prosperity. Furthermore, Birmingham had a reputation as "the most segregated city in America." **3.** The March on Washington was aimed at putting enough public pressure on Congress that it would pass what later became the Civil Rights Act of 1964.

Case Study 6

Section 1: Thinking It Over: 1. Schwerner, Chaney, and Goodman were Civil Rights workers who were murdered by white racists in Mississippi in 1964. **2.** Most African Americans were not registered to vote because racists used political, economic, and physical threats to prevent them from registering to vote.

Going to the Source: 1. Newspapers say that left-wingers and Communists are taking advantage of Northern students. **2.** The newspaper cites that the demonstrations in various cities throughout the North were organized so quickly after the murders that they must have been part of a long-term Communist plot.

Section 2: Thinking It Over: 1. Freedom Schools were schools established by Civil Rights workers in the South. They were aimed at educating African Americans and breaking the cycle of poverty that most were caught in. **2.** Answers will vary. Some students might suggest that the writer means that people will acknowledge him as an equal citizen and not just another faceless person.

Section 3: Thinking It Over: 1. When Hamer tried to register to vote she was given a literacy test and failed. She succeded on her second try. **2.** Officials gave African Americans difficult literacy tests and threatened them with violence.

Section 4: Thinking It Over: 1. The National Democratic Party offered the MFDP two seats. **2.** The MFDP rejected the compromise because it wanted full representation.

Section 5: Thinking It Over: 1. Ghettos are poor sections of a city and are often segregated. **2.** Johnson announced a "War on Poverty" in response to urban disturbances.

Case Study Review *Identifying Main Ideas:* **1.** Freedom Summer 1964 was an attempt made by Civil Rights workers from across the country to fight racism and Jim Crow laws throughout the South. **2.** African Americans learned typing, reading, and other subjects to help them gain the skills necessary to break out of the cycle of poverty. **3.** Hamer registered to vote and later led voter registration drives and joined the MFDP.

Case Study 7

Going to the Source: 1. Malcolm told his teacher that he would like to be a lawyer. Mr. Ostrowski told him being a lawyer was unrealistic for an African American and suggested that he go into carpentry. **2.** Answers will vary. Students might suggest that Malcolm felt discouraged and disappointed by this suggestion.

Section 1: Thinking It Over: 1. Marcus Garvey was an African American leader active during the first quarter of the 20th century. He argued that African Americans had to win economic, political, and cultural independence outside of white society. **2.** Malcolm fell into a life of crime in Boston and Harlem. He was involved in robbery, burglary, and drug dealing.

Section 2: Thinking It Over: 1. Malcolm took the name X because he said that his original surname, Little, was a "slave name." The "X" stood for his African name that had been lost. **2.** The Civil Rights Movement was less popular in the North than in the South because Northern African Americans already had many of the rights that were still being fought for in the South, such as the right to vote. Yet, they still lived in poverty and faced segregation and widespread prejudice in their lives.

Section 3: Thinking It Over: 1. Malcolm broke with the ideas of the Nation of Islam. He later rejected the idea that all whites were "blue-eyed devils." He also eventually recognized the improbability of forming an African American nation carved out of a number of U.S. states. **2.** Malcolm pushed Haley because he believed that he was going to be murdered. He told Haley that he did not expect to be alive to see the book published.

Case Study Review *Identifying Main Ideas:* **1.** Malcolm began to educate himself, he joined the Nation of Islam, and began to communicate with Elijah Muhammad. **2.(a)** Malcolm thought that Elijah Muhammad's teachings were a way to help African Americans improve the quality of their lives in America. **(b)** Malcolm began to question Eiljah's belief that all whites were "devils." He became convinced that the idea of a separate state was not realistic. **3.** There were significant differences. Among them: Martin Luther King, Jr., emphasized integration and equality; Malcolm and the Nation of Islam emphasized separation from whites. King believed thoroughly in nonviolence as an effective tactic. Malcolm talked about taking rights "by any means necessary," violent or non-violent.

Case Study 8

Section 1: Thinking It Over: 1. The slogan "Black Power" was first used by Stokely Carmichael during a 1966 civil rights march in Mississippi after James Meredith had been shot. **2.** According to Carmichael, integration may have helped individual African Americans, but it harmed the overall African American community and made it weaker.

Section 2: Thinking It Over: 1. There were few Jim Crow laws in the North. Discrimination generally took place outside the law. **2.** Americans were concerned. Some Americans pinpointed the cause of the riot on the poverty and lack of opportunity faced by African Americans.

Going to the Source: 1. Carmichael felt that whites had lied to African Americans because they were always told that "if you work real hard, if you sweat, if you are ambitious, then you will be successful." **2.** Carmichael believed that the white extremists who had forced African Americans to live in the ghettos were responsible for the disturbances.

Section 3: Thinking It Over: 1. Fannie Lou Hamer, a member of SNCC, believed in integration and nonviolence as essential components to winning civil rights. Stokely Carmichael rejected integration and called for the expulsion of whites from SNCC. While he did not espouse violence, he said that was a path open to African Americans. **2.** Garvey was an inspiration for the new Black Power movement. Carmichael, along with Black Power members, had studied and updated Garvey's ideas for the 1960s.

Case Study Review *Identifying Main Ideas:* **1.** It was during this march that Stokely Carmichael's call for "Black Power!" won the favor of demonstrators over Martin Luther King, Jr.'s, "Freedom Now!"slogan. **2.** The major causes were discrimination in housing, jobs, and education. Though the Northern ghettos did not have discriminatory laws, African Americans were excluded from most good housing, faced serious discrimination in jobs, and faced the likelihood of only second rate education. **3.** Martin Luther King, Jr., was the leading spokesman for civil rights demonstrations in favor of equal rights and integration. He believed in nonviolence as the best tactic for achieving these goals. The Black Power movement did not push for integration. Black Power advocates sought to control African American communities, establish African American schools, and control businesses in African American communities. Black Power advocates promoted interest in the African heritage and the study of the African American experience.

Follow-Up

Section 1: Thinking It Over: 1. Martin Luther King, Jr. was assassinated on his hotel balcony by James Earl Ray, a white racist. **2.** King meant that he could imagine the future without racism and discrimination.

Section 2: Thinking It Over: 1. Large numbers of African Americans have enrolled in service academies and broken into the top ranks in the military. **2.** Martin Luther King, Jr., opposed the Vietnam War because he said that African Americans were disproportionately affected by the war and that the war effort took resources away from the fight for equal opportunity in America.

Section 3: Thinking It Over: 1. African Americans have been elected to increasing numbers of local, state, and federal government positions. **2.** Answers will vary, but should include the fact that education is the key to putting a person into the position of securing better jobs.

Follow Up Review *Identifying Main Ideas:* **1.** Martin Luther King, Jr., opposed the U.S. role in the Vietnam War effort because he thought it took resources away from the domestic effort to gain equal opportunities for African Americans. **2.** The Civil Rights Movement made major gains in winning voting rights in areas of the South where African Americans were not permitted to vote before the beginning of the movement. **3.** African Americans played a disproportionately large role in the U.S. effort in Vietnam.

Activity Sheets

Activity Sheet 1: 1. Thursday, November 13, 1922 **2.** *The New York Times* newspaper **3.** The "shame of America" is that people were still being lynched and burnt at the stake. **4.** Between 1889 and 1922, 3,436 people were lynched. **5.** To telegraph, or contact their Senators to vote "yes" on the Dyer Anti-Lynching Bill **6.** The NAACP and the Anti-lynching Crusaders sponsored this advertisement.

Activity Sheet 2: First Paragraph: *Blue Pen* "not being able to get into a restaurant because he is Afro American" "blacks used to be banned [kept] from doing everyday activities." *Red Pen* "Today, you can easily find a restaurant owned by a black person." **Second Paragraph:** *Blue Pen* from "there weren't any black Supreme Court Justices" to "the [attacker]could get away unpunished." *Red Pen* from "maintain [hang onto] their equal status" to "we are well on our way." **Letter to the Editor** Students might include the guaranteed right to vote, desegregation of schools, African American leaders in government, or the growth of African American businesses, as some of the most important achievements of the Civil Rights Movement.

Activity Sheet 3: *The number in parentheses is the order in which the event occurred.* (6) Oliver Brown tries to register his daughter in an all-white school. (4) Levi Pearson and a group of farmers meet with Thurgood Marshall in Columbia, South Carolina. (7) Dr. Kenneth Clark testifies on the impact of segregation before the Supreme Court. (1) The Supreme Court rules on the *Plessy* v. *Ferguson* case. (5) Thurgood Marshall and top NAACP lawyers launch a plan of attack against segregation in elementary and secondary schools. (10) Thurgood Marshall becomes the first African American appointed to the Supreme Court. (2) Thurgood Marshall becomes chief counsel for the NAACP. (3) Levi Pearson and other African American parents sue Clarendon County's school board. (8) The Supreme Court rules on *Brown* v. *Board of Education.* (9) The Supreme Court orders schools to begin desegregating "with all deliberate speed." Answer to Questions: **1.** Pearson and his group went to Columbia, South Carolina, to speak to Thurgood Marshall. **2.** Oliver Brown wanted to register his daughter at the all-white school because it was closer to their home and had better facilities. **3.** Levi was suing for equal school buses; Brown was suing for desegregation. **4.** The phrase did not set specific time limits on school desegregation. The Court left it to the individual school districts to set a time table. This allowed some schools to delay desegregation for as long as they liked.

Activity Sheet 4: Students' charts might contain the following information: **Childhood:** Marshall was born in Baltimore in 1908. His father was a waiter and his mother was a teacher at a segregated school. **Early Experiences with Racism:** Students should discuss Marshall's experience as a railroad waiter. **Education:** Marshall received his law degree from Howard University. **Employment:** Marshall started working under Charles Houston, and eventually became chief counsel for NAACP. **Greatest Achievements:** Students should note both his participation in *Brown* v. *Board of Education* and his appointment to the Supreme Court. **Newspaper Article:** The newspaper article should organize the information from the chart into a descriptive article about Marshall's life.

Activity Sheet 5: 1. (a) Minniejean asked whether the white students knew anything about African Americans, or if their knowledge was limited to what their parents had told them. (b) Kay said that she had never made any effort to learn about African Americans. **2.** The white students were under pressure from their parents and friends to reject African

Americans. They had been taught that African Americans were inferior, yet they had had limited contact with African Americans and so could not judge for themselves.
3. Answers will vary, but students should explain reasons for their answers.

Activity Sheet 6: 1. Eisenhower was talking about the rioting that occurred in Little Rock in 1957 as a result of the nine African American students entering the all-white Central High School. 2. The court order said that the nine African American students should be permitted to enter the school. 3. The mobs were composed of primarily whites, with participation by some law-enforcement officials. 4. Eisenhower used federal troops because the Arkansas National Guard did nothing to stop the rioting and the harassment of the nine African American students. 5. Answers may vary, but students should support their position with facts drawn from the case study.

Activity Sheet 7: 1. The leaflet was handed out in Montgomery at the beginning of December 1955. 2. (a) The "Negro woman" is Rosa Parks. (b) Rosa Parks was not the first African American woman to be arrested for violating segregation laws on Montgomery's buses. 3. The leaflet was addressed to the African American community of Montgomery. 4. The leaflet asked everyone to boycott the bus company. 5. Answers may vary, but students should support their position. **Posters** Check students' posters for content and style.

Activity Sheet 8: Students pictures should portray the African American community of Montgomery walking to and from work. Diary entries will vary, but should include appropriate responses to the boycott.

Activity Sheet 9: 1. The people sitting at the counter are civil rights sit-in protesters. 2. They were breaking Jim Crow laws that allowed segregated lunch counters. 3. The crowd is abusing them by pouring soda and food on them and heckling them. 4. The protesters are not fighting back because they believed in nonviolence. 5. In their answers students should explain why or why not the participation of whites in the sit-ins was important.

Activity Sheet 10: 1. Clara Luper 2. Defended civil rights protesters that were arrested. 3. A student at North Carolina's A&T college, he helped organize the first sit-in in Greensboro, North Carolina. 4. Twenty-year-old student in Atlanta, Georgia, he organized huge student sit-ins in Atlanta. 5. Student Nonviolent Coordinating Committee (SNCC)

Activity Sheet 11: Possible answers. **A.** *(Second)* Martin Luther King, Jr., was arrested in Birmingham, the Southern city with the worst record of segregation. **B.** *(First)* In May 1961, James Farmer organized Freedom Rides to Alabama. **C.** *(Fourth)* The highlight of the March on Washington was Martin Luther King, Jr.'s, "I Have a Dream" speech. The March showed Congress that there was widespread support for the Civil Rights bill, which President Lyndon Johnson signed in 1964. **D.** *(Third)* Soon after President Kennedy said that he would support stronger civil rights legislation,

Medgar Evers, a civil rights activist in Jackson, Mississippi, was murdered.

Activity Sheet 12: 1. The sons of former slaves and sons of former slave owners would work together. 2. It would turn from a place of injustice and oppression into a place of freedom and justice. 3. Answers will vary, but most students will probably say that most people did agree with what King was saying. 4. Answers will vary.

Activity Sheet 13: 1. The two men are attempting to register to vote. 2. The rule that the names of people registering must be published in the newspaper. African Americans attempting to register were subjects to threats and violence if racist whites knew of their attempts. 3. Many African Americans were not able to register. 4. Answers may vary, but might relate to the lack of influence African Americans had on authorities.

Activity Sheet 14: 1. Facts: Between 1882 and 1952, Mississippi had more reported lynchings than any other state. Less than ten percent of African Americans in Mississippi voted in 1964 due to racist policies. 2. Facts: Some communities passed laws making some civil rights activities illegal. Racist groups like the Ku Klux Klan held open rallies and threatened the lives of civil rights workers. 3. Facts: Hamer was jailed and beaten by police on trumped up charges. Hamer lost her job and home when she registered to vote. 4. Facts: Mississippi Freedom Democratic Party tried to get its people named as delegates to the convention in advance. The Mississippi Freedom Democratic Party gained publicity and public sympathy at the convention in Atlantic City. 5. Facts: Most African Americans were paid less than whites for the same work. The unemployment rate for African Americans was twice that for whites.

Activity Sheet 15: Students' notes and obituaries will vary. Check for accuracy, style, grammar, and content.

Activity Sheet 16: 1. 1964 2. 1931 3. 1925 4. 1946 5. 1914 6. 1965 7. 1950 8. 1965 9. 1952 10. 1954 11. 1929 12. 1964 **Time Lines** Check students' time lines for accuracy.

Activity Sheet 17: 1. Los Angeles, San Francisco, Portland, and Tucson 2. Americus and Atlanta, Georgia; Grenada, Mississippi; Nashville, Tennessee 3. Chicago, Illinois; Dayton, Ohio; Milwaukee, Wisconsin; Detroit and Pontiac, Michigan; and Rochester, New York. 4. The Great Lakes region was the hardest hit by race riots from 1964 to 1968.

Activity Sheet 18: 1. The graph shows the change in the numbers of African American voters in certain Southern states before and after the Civil Rights Act of 1964. 2. The names of the states for which the voting information is from. 3. The number of African Americans who were registered to vote. 4. Texas had the most African American voters before the Civil Rights Act of 1964. 5. Mississippi had the least African American voters before the Civil Rights Act of 1964. 6. The largest increase in the number of African American voters occurred in Alabama.

Activity Sheet 19: 1. The graph shows the changing numbers of African American elected officials from 1970 to 1990. **2.** 1975 **3.** approximately 4,700 **4.** between 1995 and 2000 **5.** The trend shows that the number of African American elected officials has been steadily growing since 1970.

Activity Sheet 20: Students' editorials will vary, but should include information on the life of Martin Luther King, Jr. Editorials should discuss the fact that Dr. King was a leader in the Civil Rights Movement.

Tests

Overview **Matching:** 1. e 2. c 3. b 4. d 5. a
Multiple Choice: 6. c 7. d 8. a 9. c **Essay:** 10. **a.** Plessy challenged a Louisiana segregation law all the way to the Supreme Court. The Court ruled against Plessy. **b.** Wells was editor and part owner of the *Memphis Free Speech* and wrote editorials demanding justice for lynchings. **c.** Du Bois helped form the NAACP, an organization that sought to win "equal rights and opportunities for all."

Case Study 1 **Matching:** 1. d 2. a 3. b 4. c 5. e
Multiple Choice: 6. b 7. b 8. d 9. a **Essay:** 10. *Brown* v. *Board of Education* began with a suit filed by an African American named Oliver Brown. Brown tried to register his daughter in an all-white school near their home. When the school refused to allow her to register, Brown decided to sue. The case challenged a decision made by the Court in 1896 that allowed "separate but equal" to justify segregation. The Court found in favor of Brown and called for desegregation of all public schools.

Case Study 2 **Matching:** 1. c 2. d 3. e 4. b 5. a
Multiple Choice: 6. b 7. d 8. a 9. d **Essay:** 10. Students should note that the phrase the Court used was vague. Many schools in the South failed to desegregate because there were no timetables and no immediate penalties for ignoring the Court's ruling. Students might suggest that to avoid this problem the Court should have set up a timetable with penalties for schools that refused to desegregate.

Case Study 3 **Matching:** 1. c 2. b 3. e 4. a 5. d
Multiple Choice: 6. b 7. c 8. a 9. a **Essay:** 10. Rosa Parks was arrested because she violated a law that segregated whites from African Americans on Montgomery's city buses. Parks grew up in a segregated community. She could attend school for only six months in a year and had to work with her grandparents the rest of the time. Parks also heard about and witnessed the violence of the Ku Klux Klan. She believed that she had a responsibility to help end an unjust system.

Case Study 4 **Matching:** 1. d 2. b 3. c 4. a 5. e
Multiple Choice: 6. c 7. d 8. c 9. a **Essay:** 10. African American students were tired of the way they and their parents were being treated. Based on the Supreme Court's ruling in *Brown*, many were hopeful that a new era in civil rights was beginning. Students began a sit-in movement and decided that the actions they would take would be nonviolent in nature. Students founded the Student Nonviolent Coordinating Committee, (SNCC), to organize the sit-in movement.

Case Study 5 **Matching:** 1. e 2. c 3. b 4. d 5. a
Multiple Choice: 6. d 7. b 8. c 9. a **Essay:** 10. Students should recognize the role the media played in bringing images of African Americans peacefully protesting violent white mobs into people's homes. The Freedom Rides resulted in enforcement of the law that called for integrated interstate buses. The March on Washington led to the passage of the Civil Rights Act.

Case Study 6 **Matching:** 1. d 2. a 3. c 4. b 5. e
Multiple Choice: 6. d 7. a 8. b 9. a **Essay:** 10. **a.** Cause: racism; Effect: outrage and determination to fight for civil rights in the South. **b.** Cause: equal education had been denied to African Americans; Effect: African Americans began learning about black history and about their rights as U.S. citizens. **c.** Cause: segregation in the regular Democratic Party excluded African Americans from participating; Effect: Integration of African Americans and whites in future Democratic party conventions. **d.** Cause: discrimination and the poor living conditions of African Americans in Northern cities are ignored by the government; Effect: President Johnson announces a "War on Poverty."

Case Study 7 **Matching:** 1. d 2. e 3. c 4. a 5. b
Multiple Choice: 6. a 7. b 8. c 9. a **Essay:** 10. Students should recognize that the main change in Malcolm X's views was his feelings about the roots of racism in the United States and his feelings toward whites.

Case Study 8 **Matching:** 1. c 2. a 3. e 4. b 5. d
Multiple Choice: 6. b 7. d 8. a 9. c **Essay:** 10. King advocated integration of whites and African Americans. Carmichael advocated separation. Students should cite facts from the case study to support their answers.

Follow-Up **Matching:** 1. b 2. a 3. d 4. e 5. c
Multiple Choice: 6. a 7. c 8. a 9. d **Essay:** 10. Students' responses will vary. The Civil Rights Movement helped achieve the right to vote for African Americans. There is no longer legal segregation of public facilities. Students may also note that African Americans have started to gain seats in both our state and federal governments. Discrimination still exists in hiring practices and pay scales, and institutional racism still exists.

Activity Sheet 1: Analyzing an Advertisement

Name: _____ **Date:** _____

Overview: The Civil Rights Struggle

Advertisements that appear in newspapers and magazines can provide valuable information about the time in which they first appeared. Study the advertisement that appears below. Review the information contained in the Overview on text pages 5–10. Then answer the questions at the bottom of this activity sheet.

> *THE NEW YORK TIMES, THURSDAY, NOVEMBER 13, 1922*
>
> ## THE SHAME OF AMERICA
>
> Do you know that the <u>United States</u> is the <u>Only Land on Earth</u>
> where human beings are
> **<u>BURNED AT THE STAKE?</u>**
>
> In Four Years, 1918–1921, twenty-eight People Were Publicly
> **BURNED BY AMERICAN MOBS**
> 3,436 People Lynched 1889 to 1922
> AND THE LYNCHERS GO UNPUNISHED
>
> **THE REMEDY:**
> The **DYER ANTI-LYNCHING BILL** is now
> before the UNITED STATES SENATE.
> <u>TELEGRAPH YOUR SENATORS TODAY</u> IF YOU WANT IT ENACTED.
>
> NATIONAL ASSOCIATION FOR THE ADVANCEMENT OF COLORED PEOPLE
> 36 Fifth Avenue, New York City
> This Advertisement Is Paid for in Part by the Anti-lynching Crusaders

1. When did this advertisement first appear?

_____

2. Where did it appear?

_____

3. According to the advertisement, what is the "shame of America"?

_____

_____

4. How many people were killed by violent mobs between 1889 and 1922?

_____

5. What action did the advertisement ask readers to take to stop the violence?

_____

6. What two organizations paid for this advertisement?

_____

Activity Sheet 2: Comparing Past and Present

Name: _____ **Date:** _____

Overview: The Civil Rights Struggle

February is Black History Month in the United States. It is a time to celebrate and focus on the progress made by African Americans. In February 1988, the *Washington Post* asked African American students to write letters about how the Civil Rights Movement had changed their lives. The excerpt below is one of the students' letters printed by the newspaper. Read this letter carefully. Using a blue pen, underline sentences that show the way things were at the start of the Civil Rights Movement. Using a red pen, underline sentences that show how things have changed. Then, write a letter that you might send to your local newspaper during Black History Month. Explain what you think the most important successes of the Civil Rights Movement have been over the years.

My dad has told me of not being able to get into a restaurant because he is an Afro-American. I have seen stories on television of how blacks used to be banned [kept] from doing everyday activities. Today, you can easily find a restaurant owned by a black person.

At the beginning of the Civil Rights Movement, there weren't any black Supreme Court Justices. There weren't any black people running for President. A black man could be beaten up in his own home and the [attacker] could get away unpunished.

The accomplishments in the last 25 years are remarkable [amazing]. What is equally important is the determination [strong desire] for black people to maintain [hang onto] their equal status [position in society]. Although we have not reached the totally integrated [racially mixed] society that Martin Luther King, Jr., and others dreamed of, we are well on our way.

Dear Editor:

_____

_____

_____

_____

_____

_____

_____

                                    Sincerely,

Activity Sheet 3: Understanding Chronology

Name: _____ **Date:** _____

Case Study 1: Jim Crow Is Expelled from School

The list of events below relate to school desegregation. The events are **not** in chronological order. Read the list and decide which event came first, then second, and so on. Then in the spaces next to the events, number the events in the order in which they occurred. After you have put the events in chronological order, answer the questions that follow.

_____ Oliver Brown tries to register his daughter in an all-white school.

_____ Levi Pearson and a group of farmers meet with Thurgood Marshall in Columbia, South Carolina.

_____ Dr. Kenneth Clark testifies on the impact of segregation on children before the Supreme Court.

_____ The Supreme Court rules on the *Plessy* v. *Ferguson* case.

_____ Thurgood Marshall and top NAACP lawyers launch a plan of attack against segregation in elementary and secondary schools.

_____ Thurgood Marshall becomes the first African American appointed to the Supreme Court.

_____ Thurgood Marshall becomes chief counsel for the NAACP.

_____ Levi Pearson and other African American parents sue Clarendon County's school board.

_____ The Supreme Court rules on *Brown* v. *Board of Education*.

_____ The Supreme Court orders schools to begin desegregating "with all deliberate speed."

1. What happened after Levi Pearson sued the Clarendon County school board for equal busing for African American students?

_____

2. Why did Oliver Brown try to register his daughter in an all-white school?

_____

3. What was the major difference between the case that Levi Pearson brought before Clarendon County Court and the case Oliver Brown brought before the Supreme Court?

_____

4. The Supreme Court ordered schools to desegregate "with all deliberate speed." What problems did the phrase "with all deliberate speed" cause?

_____

_____

Activity Sheet 4: Organizing Personal Information

Name: _____ **Date:** _____

Case Study 1: Jim Crow Is Expelled from School

Pretend that you are a reporter for a newspaper. It is 1954 and you have been covering the Supreme Court Case of *Brown* v. *Board of Education*. You have been asked to write a short article on the background of Thurgood Marshall. Fill in the chart below with some of the personal information that you obtained about Marshall in Case Study 1. Then, using the completed chart, organize the information into a clear newspaper article detailing Marshall's life and achievements.

Childhood	
Early Experiences with Racism	
Education	
Employment	
Greatest Achievements	

Thurgood Marshall In-Depth

by: _____

_____

_____

_____

_____

_____

_____

_____

_____

Activity Sheet 5: Analyzing Primary Sources

Name: _____ **Date:** _____

Case Study 2: The Mob at Central High School

Just weeks after the Little Rock Nine started at Central High School, a roundtable discussion was held between white and African American students at Central. Kay, Joe, Robin, and Sammy were white participants in the discussion; Ernest and Minniejean were African American students in the discussion. Mrs. Ricketts was the moderator. Below is an excerpt from that discussion. Read the excerpt and answer the questions that follow.

Minniejean: Kay, Joe, and Robin—do you know anything about me, or is it just that your mother has told you about Negroes?

Mrs. Ricketts: Have you ever really made an effort to try to find out what they're like?

Kay: Not until today.

Sammy: Not until today.

Mrs. Ricketts: And what do you think about it after today?

Kay: Well, you know that my parents and a lot of the other students and their parents think that Negroes aren't equal to us. But—I don't know. It seems like they are, to me.

Sammy: These people are—we'll have to admit that.

More discussion followed, in which all agreed that sitting down and talking about their differences was the best way to resolve the conflict. The discussion ended on a positive note:

Kay: We [Sammy and I] both came down here today with our minds set on it [that] we weren't going to change our minds that we were fully against integration. But I know now that we're going to change our minds.

1. (a) What question did Minniejean ask the white students? (b) What answer did Kay give Minniejean?

_____

_____

2. Why do you think it was difficult for white students like Kay and Sammy to accept integration in their school?

_____

_____

3. Imagine that you were a white student at Central High in 1957. What position do you think you would have taken on the issue of integration? Explain.

_____

_____

_____

Activity Sheet 6: Interpreting a Primary Source

Name: _____ Date: _____

Case Study 2: The Mob at Central High School

Although the *Brown* v. *Board of Education* case (1954) outlawed segregation in schools, it did not lead to immediate integration. Many whites in the deep South resented the Court's decision. The experience of the Little Rock Nine in 1957 is an example of this resentment boiling over into violence. Below is an excerpt from the speech President Eisenhower gave when he nationalized the Arkansas National Guard. Read the excerpt and answer the questions that follow.

> *For a few minutes this evening I want to talk to you about the serious situation that has arisen in Little Rock. . . . In that city . . . disorderly [uncontrollable] mobs have deliberately [on purpose] prevented the carrying out of proper orders from a federal court. Local authorities have not eliminated that violent opposition and, under the law, I yesterday issued a proclamation [statement] calling upon the mob to disperse [go away]. In accordance with my responsibility, I have today issued an executive order directing the use of troops under federal authority to aid in the execution [carrying out] of federal law at Little Rock, Arkansas. If resistance to the federal court order ceases [stops] at once, the further presence of federal troops will be unnecessary and the city of Little Rock will return to its normal habits of peace and order.*

1. What was the "serious situation" that Eisenhower was talking about?

_____

_____

2. What court order was the mob defying?

_____

_____

3. Who were the people in the "disorderly mobs"?

_____

4. Why was Eisenhower forced to use *federal* troops instead of *state* troops?

_____

5. If you had been in Eisenhower's position, would you have sent in federal troops? Why or why not?

_____

_____

Activity Sheet 7: Interpreting a Leaflet

Name: _____ **Date:** _____

Case Study 3: Rosa Parks and the Montgomery Bus Boycott

After Rosa Parks was arrested for violating the city of Montgomery's segregation laws, the African American community decided to stage a bus boycott. The leaflet below was handed out in December 1955, the weekend after Rosa Parks was arrested. Read the leaflet and review Case Study 3. Then answer the questions that follow.

DON'T RIDE THE BUS to work, to town, to school, or any place **MONDAY, DECEMBER 5.**

Another Negro woman has been arrested and put in jail because she refused to give up her bus seat.

Don't ride the buses to work, to school, or anywhere on Monday. If you work, take a cab, or share a ride.

Come to a mass meeting, Monday at 7:00 p.m., at the Holt Street Baptist Church for further instruction.

---

1. Where and when was the leaflet handed out?

_____

2. (a) What is the name of the "Negro woman" referred to in the leaflet?

_____

(b) What can you infer or guess from the words "Another Negro woman"?

_____

3. To whom do you think the leaflet is addressed? Why do you think so?

_____

4. What action does the leaflet call for?

_____

_____

5. What statements in the leaflet were the most convincing? Explain your answer.

_____

_____

On a separate sheet of paper, design a poster that you think would convince people to take the action that the leaflet calls for.

Activity Sheet 8: Understanding Historical Events

Name: _____ **Date:** _____

Case Study 3: Rosa Parks and the Montgomery Bus Boycott

Read the subsection *The Walking City* on page 45 of your text. Pretend that you were one of the boycotters, forced to walk to and from work every day. In the space below, draw a picture of what the roads along Montgomery's bus routes might have looked like during the bus boycott in 1956. Then, write a diary entry describing your feelings about what you have witnessed on the road as you walked to work.

Date: _____

Dear Diary,

_____

_____

_____

_____

_____

_____

Activity Sheet 9: Analyzing a Photograph

Name: _____ **Date:** _____

Case Study 4: Sitting In for Justice

Protesters who took part in the sit-ins of the 1960s believed in the power of civil disobedience. Civil disobedience is the act of breaking a law that one believes is unjust. The protesters also believed in nonviolence. This meant that although they were often abused and attacked, sit-in participants refused to fight back. The picture below was taken during a sit-in in Jackson, Mississippi. Study the picture and answer the questions that follow.

1. Who are the people sitting at the counter?

_____

2. What law are these people breaking?

_____

3. What is the crowd doing to the people at the counter?

_____

4. Why do you think the protesters are not fighting back?

_____

5. Whites as well as blacks were involved in the sit-ins. Do you think the involvement of whites was important? Explain your answer.

_____

_____

_____

Activity Sheet 10: Organizing Historical Information into a Chart

Name: _____ **Date:** _____

Case Study 4: Sitting In for Justice

Making a chart is a good way to organize information about different groups. In this case study, you read about individuals and groups that played important roles in the Civil Rights Movement during the early 1960s. Skim through the case study again to complete the chart below. Some of the entries have been made already.

Group or Individual	Importance to Sit-ins
1.	Led the first sit-ins in Oklahoma City. Although they were unsuccessful, she opened the path for the more successful sit-ins of the 1960s.
2. NAACP	
3. Ezell Blair, Jr.	
4. Julian Bond	
5.	Organization that gave protesters lessons in nonviolence. Taught protesters how to protect themselves if they were beaten. Gave legal help to protesters who were arrested.

Activity Sheet 11: Organizing Ideas and Chronology

Name: _____ **Date:** _____

Case Study 5: Freedom Rides and Freedom Marches

History is made up of people, places, and things interacting with each other. This exercise will help you think about how some things came together in the years leading up to and during the Civil Rights Movement of the 1950s and 1960s.

    Below you will see clusters of terms. Use the terms in each cluster to write a sentence or two on the lines provided about an event during the Civil Rights Movement. After you have written four sentences, number them in the order in which the events took place.

Order

_____ **A.** Birmingham   Arrest   Segregation   Martin Luther King, Jr.

    _____

    _____

    _____

_____ **B.** Freedom Ride   James Farmer   Alabama   May 1961

    _____

    _____

    _____

_____ **C.** March on Washington   "I Have a Dream"   Lyndon Johnson
Civil Rights Act

    _____

    _____

    _____

_____ **D.** John F. Kennedy   Medgar Evers   Civil Rights   Jackson, Mississippi

    _____

    _____

    _____

Activity Sheet 12: Interpreting Primary Sources

Name: _____ Date: _____

Case Study 5: Freedom Rides and Freedom Marches

During the March on Washington in August 1963, Martin Luther King, Jr., gave a speech that has come to be known as the "I Have a Dream" speech. In the speech, Dr. King tried to explain his dream of a United States where everyone experienced equality and freedom. Read the excerpt below and then answer the questions. In the space provided, write how you would have felt hearing this speech if you had been in Washington in August 1963.

I say to you today, my friends, that in spite of the difficulties and frustrations of the moment, I still have a dream. It is a dream deeply rooted in the American dream.

I have a dream that one day on the red hills of Georgia the sons of former slaves and the sons of former slave owners will be able to sit down together at a table of brotherhood.

I have a dream that one day even the state of Mississippi, a desert state, sweltering with the heat of injustice and oppression, will be transformed into an oasis [wonderful place] of freedom and justice.

I have a dream that my four children will one day live in a nation where they will not be judged by the color of their skin but by the content of their character.

I have a dream today.

1. What did Martin Luther King, Jr., hope would happen in Georgia?

_____

2. What were Dr. King's hopes for the state of Mississippi?

_____

3. Do you think most people who attended the March on Washington hoped for the same things that Dr. King did? Explain.

_____

_____

4. Pretend that you attended the March on Washington in 1963. You are riding home with your friends and discussing Dr. King's speech. You decide to add to Dr. King's list of dreams one or two of your own dreams for the Civil Rights Movement. What dreams of your own might you add?

_____

_____

_____

Activity Sheet 13: Interpreting a Photograph

Name: _____   **Date:** _____

Case Study 6: Facing Jim Crow Laws

African Americans who wanted to vote faced many laws that were designed to prevent them from successfully registering. Literacy tests were used to exclude African Americans from voting. Easy literacy tests were given to whites, while African Americans were given difficult tests. The picture below shows an early attempt by African Americans to register in Mississippi. Study the photograph and the sign in the picture and answer the questions below.

1. What are the two African American men at the counter doing?

_____

2. What rules in the sign make registering difficult or dangerous for African Americans?

_____

_____

3. How do you think these rules affected African Americans?

_____

_____

4. How do you think not being able to vote affected the African American community?

_____

_____

_____

Activity Sheet 14: Supplying Supporting Evidence

Name: _____   Date: _____

Case Study 6: Freedom Summer, 1964

Read each of the main ideas listed below. Use Case Study 6 to help you supply at least two facts to support each main idea.

1. **Main Idea:** Of all the states in the South, Mississippi was the place most in need of civil rights reform.

   Fact: _____

   Fact: _____

2. **Main Idea:** The people who volunteered to work in Mississippi during Freedom Summer faced a number of obstacles.

   Fact: _____

   Fact: _____

3. **Main Idea:** Fannie Lou Hamer risked a great deal to fight for civil rights for herself and other African Americans.

   Fact: _____

   Fact: _____

4. **Main Idea:** The Mississippi Freedom Democratic Party challenged the whites-only Democratic party in Mississippi at the 1964 Democratic National Convention.

   Fact: _____

   Fact: _____

5. **Main Idea:** Although there were no Jim Crow laws in the North, African Americans who lived there felt the sting of racism and segregation.

   Fact: _____

   Fact: _____

Activity Sheet 15: Writing a Remembrance

Name: _____   **Date:** _____

Case Study 7: The Bitter Struggle of Malcolm X

On February 21, 1965, Malcolm X was murdered at the age of 40. He had spent nearly half his life preaching the teachings of Elijah Muhammad and trying to gain recruits for the Nation of Islam. Pretend that you are a newspaper reporter. You have just been assigned to write a **remembrance** on Malcolm X. It should be a short biography of the person that has died.

   Below are some notes on Malcolm X's early life. Like notes taken in research, they are written in incomplete sentences. Study these notes. Then add some other interesting facts about Malcolm X that you read about in the case study. Use these notes to write an remembrance on the lines below.

Background Notes	Additional Notes
Born in 1925 in Omaha, Nebraska.	
Fourth of eight children.	
Father was a minister and follower of Marcus Garvey.	
Converted to Islam in jail and joined the Nation of Islam under Elijah Muhammad.	
Recruited African Americans into the Nation of Islam and spoke at rallies preaching self-advancement, not reliance on white society.	

_____ **(Headline)**

February 22, 1965

*Story by*_____

_____

_____

_____

_____

_____

Activity Sheet 16: Making a Time Line

Name: _____ Date: _____

Case Study 7: The Bitter Struggle of Malcolm X

Below is a list of 12 key events in the life of Malcolm X. First, using the list of dates, match the events and the years in which they occurred. You may use a date more than once. Next, on the back of this worksheet or on a separate sheet of paper, draw a long line and place each event and date in chronological order. You may also add any other historical events that you believe are important. On your time line, include a brief description of the event and its significance in the life of Malcolm X. Refer to your text for help.

Events

_____ **1.** Malcolm X leaves the Nation of Islam.

_____ **2.** Earl Little dies.

_____ **3.** Malcolm Little is born.

_____ **4.** Malcolm Little is arrested.

_____ **5.** Marcus Garvey begins the Universal Negro Improvement Association (UNIA).

_____ **6.** Malcolm X is assassinated

_____ **7.** Malcolm Little joins the Nation of Islam and changes his last name to "X."

_____ **8.** Malcolm X announces a new slogan "Ballots or bullets."

_____ **9.** Malcolm X is released from prison.

_____ **10.** Malcolm X moves to Boston to recruit members for the Nation of Islam.

_____ **11.** The Little family's house in Lansing Michigan is burned down.

_____ **12.** Malcolm X travels to Saudi Arabia and Africa.

Dates

1914   1925   1929   1931   1946   1950   1952   1954   1964   1965

Activity Sheet 17: Interpreting a Chart

Name: _____ **Date:** _____

Case Study 8: Black Power!

The struggle over Civil Rights became more intense and more violent throughout the late 1960s. For a time, national attention focused on the sit-ins and Freedom Rides in the South. But Senator Robert Kennedy predicted that trouble was brewing elsewhere in the country. "Cities where blacks are trapped in pockets of poverty—Harlem, Watts, South Side [Chicago]—are riots just waiting to happen," he said. From 1965 to 1968, cities across the nation exploded. The chart on this page shows where the largest riots took place. Using this chart and a map of the United States, answer the questions that follow.

Civil Rights Riots, 1965–1968

Cities with riots	Outcome	Cities with riots	Outcome
Americus, Georgia	fatalities	Milwaukee, Wisconsin	fatalities
Atlanta, Georgia	fatalities	Nashville, Tennessee	fatalities
Boston, Massachusetts	fatalities	New York, New York	fatalities
Chicago, Illinois	fatalities	Newark, New Jersey	fatalities
Cincinnati, Ohio	fatalities	Philadelphia, Pennsylvania	fatalities
Cleveland, Ohio	fatalities	Pontiac, Michigan	fatalities
Dayton, Ohio	fatalities	Portland, Oregon	fatalities
Detroit, Michigan	fatalities	Rochester, New York	fatalities
Grenada, Mississippi	fatalities	San Francisco, California	fatalities
Kansas City, Missouri	fatalities	Tampa, Florida	fatalities
Los Angeles, California	fatalities	Tucson, Arizona	fatalities
Louisville, Kentucky	fatalities	Washington, D.C.	fatalities

1. In what major western cities did riots occur?

_____

2. In what major cities of the South did riots occur?

_____

3. In what cities along the Great Lakes did people die during the rioting?

_____

4. What region saw the most civil rights rioting from 1965 to 1968?

_____

Activity Sheet 18: Reading a Bar Graph

Name: _____ Date: _____

Case Study 8: Black Power!

Graphs organize statistical information in an easy-to-read diagram. The graph on this page is called a *bar graph* because it uses bars to show amounts. To practice your graph skills, study the graph below. Then answer the questions that follow. The *map key* in the upper right hand corner of the graph shows the difference between the two different color bars.

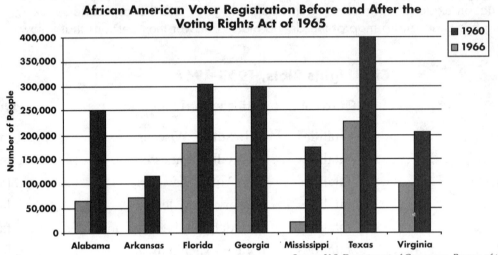

African American Voter Registration Before and After the Voting Rights Act of 1965

Source: U.S. Department of Commerce, Bureau of the Census, Statistical Abstract of the United States: 1982–83, 103rd Edition.

1. What is the subject of this graph?

_____

2. The **horizontal axis** is the line on the graph that runs sideways across the bottom of the graph. What information is on the horizontal axis?

_____

3. The **vertical axis** is the line on the graph that runs up and down on the left side of the graph. What information is on the vertical axis?

_____

4. Which state had the most African American voters before the Civil Rights Act of 1964? (Hint: Look at the **map key**.)

_____

5. Which state had the least African American voters before the Civil Rights Act of 1964?

_____

6. Which state had the largest increase in the number of African American voters?

_____

Activity Sheet 19: Reading a Line Graph

Name: _____ **Date:** _____

Follow-Up: The Road Partly Traveled

Graphs organize statistical information in an easy-to-read diagram. The graph on this page is called a *line graph* because it uses indicator lines to show amounts. To practice your graph skills, study the graph below. It shows the number of African Americans elected to office from 1970 to 1990. Then answer the questions that follow.

African American Elected Officials, 1970–1990

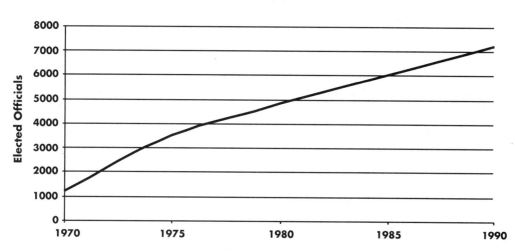

Officials include members of the U.S. Congress; state senators and representatives; county commissioners and supervisors; city mayors, council members, and alderpersons; judges, magistrates, justices of the peace and constables; and members of college and local school boards.

Source: Joint Center for Political & Economic Studies, "Black Elected Officials" (Washington, D.C.)

1. What information does the graph show?

_____

2. Around what year did the number of African American elected officials reach 3,500?

_____

3. Approximately how many African American elected officials were there in 1980?

_____

4. Based on this graph, what year do you think the number of African American elected officials will reach 8,000?

_____

5. What pattern does the graph illustrate?

_____

_____

Activity Sheet 20: Writing an Editorial

Name: _____ **Date:** _____

Follow-Up: The Road Partly Traveled

Pretend that it is April 4, 1968. You are a newspaper reporter in Memphis, Tennessee. Originally, you were supposed to write an article about Martin Luther King, Jr.'s Poor People's Campaign. Yesterday, however, as he stood on the balcony of his hotel, King was murdered. Now, you must write an editorial talking about Martin Luther King, Jr., and his contributions to the Civil Rights Movement. An editorial is an article that expresses a writer's personal opinions on a subject. Use the information in the chart below along with data you have collected from your reading to discuss Martin Luther King, Jr., and his contributions to the Civil Rights Movement. Write your editorial on a separate sheet of paper.

Background Information	Additional Notes
Born January 15, 1929, in Atlanta, Georgia. Father and grandfather were Baptist ministers.	
Graduated from Morehouse College. Ordained a minister in 1947.	
Began civil rights crusade in 1955. He led boycotts, marches, and sit-ins throughout the South.	
Led march on Washington on April 28, 1963.	
Awarded Nobel Prize in 1964.	
Murdered April 4, 1968.	

_____ **(Headline)**

April 4, 1968   Memphis, Tennessee

Story by _____

_____

_____

_____

_____

Overview Test: The Civil Rights Struggle

Name: _____ **Date:** _____

I. Matching Decide which definition in the right column best explains a term in the left column. Then write the letter of that definition in the space next to the term.

_____ 1. segregation

_____ 2. discriminate

_____ 3. civil rights

_____ 4. ghetto

_____ 5. lynching

a. hanging or otherwise murdering by mob action without a lawful trial

b. rights given to U.S. citizens and protected by the Constitution

c. to treat someone in a different way based on their race, religion, or sex

d. a poor section of a city where a particular group is forced to live

e. separation of people by race

II. Multiple Choice Choose the answer that best completes the sentence or answers the question. Then write the letter of your choice in the space provided.

_____ 6. The Fourteenth Amendment to the Constitution says

a. that all U.S. citizens have the right to bear arms.

b. that all U.S. citizens deserve a fair trial in front of a jury.

c. that all U.S. citizens are guaranteed equal protection under the law.

d. that all U.S. citizens have the right to vote, regardless of race or sex.

_____ 7. The 1896 Supreme Court case *Plessy* v. *Ferguson*

a. gave African Americans the right to sit anywhere they pleased on public transportation.

b. guaranteed equal job opportunities for African Americans.

c. allowed African Americans to play professional baseball.

d. upheld segregation and the idea of "separate but equal."

_____ 8. The Great Migration was

a. the movement of large numbers of African Americans to the North during the early 1900s.

b. a civil rights march led by Dr. Martin Luther King, Jr.

c. the name of an African American bus company.

d. an increase in the number of white participants in the Civil Rights Movement.

_____ 9. The National Association for the Advancement of Colored People (NAACP)

a. was founded by Martin Luther King, Jr.

b. was formed before the Civil War to protect blacks in the South.

c. wanted to win equal rights and opportunities for all African Americans.

d. supported the idea of "separate but equal."

III. Essay Write your answer to the following in paragraph form on a separate piece of paper.

_____ 10. Before the Civil Rights Movement of the 1960s began, many African Americans fought for racial equality in the United States. Choose two of the following people and describe the actions that each took to fight for equal rights for African Americans: **a.** Homer A. Plessy **b.** Ida B. Wells **c.** W.E.B. Du Bois.

Case Study 1 Test: Jim Crow Is Expelled from School

Name: _____ Date: _____

I. Matching
Decide which definition in the right column best explains a term in the left column. Then write the letter of that definition in the space next to the term.

___ 1. integrate

___ 2. psychology

___ 3. unanimous

___ 4. desegregate

___ 5. poll tax

a. the study of the human mind and behavior

b. complete or total agreement in a group

c. to legally end separation by race

d. to bring together

e. a tax some states required citizens to pay in order to vote

II. Multiple Choice
Choose the answer that best completes the sentence or answers the question. Then write the letter of your choice in the space provided.

___ 6. The state of Alabama spent

a. about equal amounts of money on white and African American students.

b. more money on white students.

c. more money on African American students.

d. a great deal of money to make schools for African American students equal to schools for whites.

___ 7. One method used by the NAACP to fight legal segregation of school districts was

a. to use violence.

b. to bring suits against specific school districts.

c. to stage boycotts in front of the schools.

d. to send African American students to non-segregated schools in the North.

___ 8. All of the following were arguments used by supporters of segregation *except*

a. The Constitution did not give the federal government the power to run schools.

b. It was up to the states to decide whether or not to keep school systems segregated.

c. Local governments were better able to determine what kind of education parents wanted than the federal government.

d. The federal government was better able to determine what kind of education parents wanted than the state governments.

___ 9. Dr. Kenneth Clark

a. was a very important witness in the *Brown* v. *Board of Education* case.

b. felt that racially segregated schools helped children learn.

c. testified on behalf of Southern school districts in favor of segregation.

d. All of the above.

III. Essay
Write your answer to the following in paragraph form on a separate piece of paper.

10. *Brown* v. *Board of Education* (1954) was a landmark case in the fight for African American civil rights. Discuss the events that led up to the *Brown* v. *Board of Education* case and the issues with which it dealt. What did the Court decide in *Brown* v. *Board of Education*?

Case Study 2 Test: The Mob at Central High School

Name: _____ Date: _____

I. Matching
Decide which definition in the right column best explains a term in the left column. Then write the letter of that definition in the space next to the term.

____ 1. propaganda

____ 2. manifesto

____ 3. federalize

____ 4. outside agitators

____ 5. White Citizens' Councils

a. groups that were formed in the South and that promised to oppose integration in every community

b. people from outside of a community who try to start trouble

c. the spreading of ideas in order to shape people's opinions

d. a statement of beliefs

e. to put under the control of the national government

II. Multiple Choice
Choose the answer that best completes the sentence or answers the question. Then write the letter of your choice in the space provided.

____ 6. The Little Rock Nine were

a. a group of students who were against desegregating Central High School.

b. the first African American students to attend Central High School.

c. the name of the military division that helped desegregate Central High School.

d. members of the Board of Education of Central High School.

____ 7. When it came to integrating public schools, Governor Orval Faubus believed that Arkansas should

a. spend more money on African American schools.

b. integrate with all deliberate speed.

c. help African Americans to attend Central High School.

d. oppose the Supreme Court's ruling on integration.

____ 8. President Eisenhower decided to federalize the Arkansas National Guard after

a. mobs in Little Rock rioted.

b. Governor Faubus said he would allow integration.

c. a rock was thrown through Daisy Bates's window.

d. Elizabeth Eckford was attacked on the way to Central High School.

____ 9. All the following statements below are correct except

a. Elizabeth Huckaby was disappointed when African Americans were turned away at the doors of the school.

b. Melba Pattillo and her family were threatened the night before she was to attend Central High School.

c. Protected by the U.S. Army, the African American students were able to attend Central High School.

d. the White Citizens' Councils were formed to protect African Americans' right to attend all-white high schools.

III. Essay
Write your answer to the following in paragraph form on a separate piece of paper.

10. In the *Brown* v. *Board of Education* (1954) case, the Supreme Court ruled that all school districts must desegregate "with all deliberate speed." What problems did the phrase "with all deliberate speed" cause? What words might the Court have used to eliminate those problems? Explain your answer.

Case Study 3 Test: Rosa Parks and the Montgomery Bus Boycott

Name: _____   **Date:** _____

I. Matching Decide which definition in the right column best explains a term in the left column. Then write the letter of that definition in the space next to the term.

____ 1. donation

____ 2. theology

____ 3. nonviolence

____ 4. injustice

____ 5. protest

a. something done in an unfair manner

b. the study of religion

c. money given to help a group with their cause

d. speak or act in opposition to something

e. the peaceful refusal to obey unjust laws

II. Multiple Choice Choose the answer that best completes the sentence or answers the question. Then write the letter of your choice in the space provided.

____ 6. When Martin Luther King, Jr., was offered a post at the Dexter Avenue Baptist Church in 1955, he and his wife

a. agreed to fight to preserve segregation.

b. decided to accept the post because they believed that "something remarkable was about to happen."

c. decided to remain in Boston until the South was integrated.

d. believed Rosa Parks should be jailed.

____ 7. The Southern Christian Leadership Conference (SCLC)

a. was an organization of religious leaders fighting for segregation.

b. was under the leadership of Thurgood Marshall and Rosa Parks.

c. relied on nonviolent protest.

d. was formed during the Civil War to protect African Americans.

____ 8. The Montgomery bus boycott

a. nearly crippled the Montgomery Bus Company.

b. was only partially successful.

c. began in 1953.

d. lasted less than two months.

____ 9. Rosa Parks

a. was arrested for not giving her seat to a white person.

b. protested against the Montgomery bus boycott.

c. led the movement to gain the vote for women during the 1920s.

d. testified before the Supreme Court during the *Brown* v. *Board of Education* case.

III. Essay Write your answer to the following in paragraph form on a separate piece of paper.

10. Why was Rosa Parks arrested December 1, 1955? Why do you think Parks agreed to allow her arrest to be used as an example to start the Montgomery bus boycott? Discuss how Parks's experiences as a child growing up in a segregated system might have affected the decision she made.

Case Study 4 Test: Sitting In for Justice

Name: _____ Date: _____

I. Matching Decide which definition in the right column best explains a term in the left column. Then write the letter of that definition in the space next to the term.

____ 1. civil disobedience

____ 2. spirituals

____ 3. SNCC

____ 4. picket

____ 5. sit-in

a. to walk or assemble outside a place to publicize a cause

b. songs that originated during slavery

c. an organization that coordinated student protests

d. the act of breaking a law that a person thinks is unjust using nonviolent methods

e. a type of protest

II. Multiple Choice Choose the answer that best completes the sentence or answers the question. Then write the letter of your choice in the space provided.

____ 6. The first of the successful sit-ins of the 1960s occurred in

a. New York City.

b. Topeka, Kansas.

c. Greensboro, North Carolina.

d. Little Rock, Arkansas.

____ 7. In 1960, more than _____ percent of African American students in the South attended separate schools.

a. 15

b. 30

c. 80

d. 99

____ 8. Thurgood Marshall

a. felt that civil disobedience as a form of protest should be avoided at all cost.

b. said African Americans should ignore segregation in stores.

c. eventually supported sit-ins as a method of protest.

d. felt that African Americans should stop pushing for integration.

____ 9. Eventually, white merchants in the South

a. decided that integration was good business and began to open their doors to African American customers.

b. swore never to cave in to the demands of the sit-in protesters.

c. allowed African Americans into their businesses, but refused to serve them.

d. closed their stores rather than serve African Americans.

III. Essay Write your answer to the following in paragraph form on a separate piece of paper.

10. Explain the role of students in the sit-in movement. How and why did students start the movement? How did they keep it going? What is the SNCC and how did it support the sit-in movement?

Case Study 5 Test: Freedom Rides and Freedom Marches

Name: _____ Date: _____

I. Matching Decide which definition in the right column best explains a term in the left column. Then write the letter of that definition in the space next to the term.

____ 1. Freedom Rides

____ 2. reconciliation

____ 3. suits

____ 4. interstate

____ 5. bigot

a. a person who is intolerant of other races

b. legal cases

c. to make friendly again

d. between or across state lines

e. protests against segregation on interstate buses in the South

II. Multiple Choice Choose the answer that best completes the sentence or answers the question. Then write the letter of your choice in the space provided.

____ 6. Protesters who took part in the Freedom Rides

a. faced no personal danger.

b. were all African Americans.

c. felt that continued segregation was good for both whites and African Americans.

d. risked being beaten, arrested, or even killed.

____ 7. The federal government

a. was eager to get involved in protecting the Freedom Riders.

b. was reluctant to get involved on behalf of the Freedom Riders.

c. protected the Freedom Riders from the beginning of the protests.

d. organized the Freedom Rides.

____ 8. Martin Luther King, Jr.'s, "Letter from a Birmingham Jail" was

a. written to protest the miserable conditions in Southern jails.

b. an attempt to raise money for the Civil Rights Movement.

c. in response to a letter written by eight white ministers from Alabama.

d. none of the above.

____ 9. Medgar Evers was

a. an NAACP official who was murdered in Mississippi.

b. the man who shot John F. Kennedy.

c. a Congressman from Alabama who helped get the Civil Rights Act passed.

d. the leader of the Freedom Rides.

III. Essay Write your answer to the following in paragraph form on a separate piece of paper.

10. What role did television, radio, and newspapers play in the successes of the Freedom Rides and marches of the early 1960s? Discuss how the media affected the outcomes of these events. Then discuss at least two results of the Freedom Rides and marches.

Case Study 6 Test: Freedom Summer, 1964

Name: _____ Date: _____

I. Matching Decide which definition in the right column best explains a term in the left column. Then write the letter of that definition in the space next to the term.

____ 1. unseat

____ 2. compromise

____ 3. delegate

____ 4. convention

____ 5. literacy test

a. an agreement where both sides give in a little

b. a meeting of members of a group

c. a person acting as another's representative

d. to replace a person in political office

e. a test that is supposed to measure a person's ability to read and write

II. Multiple Choice Choose the answer that best completes the sentence or answers the question. Then write the letter of your choice in the space provided.

____ 6. Some of the goals of Freedom Summer 1964 were

a. to register more African Americans to vote.

b. to increase the country's awareness of the situation in the deep South.

c. to decrease the power of white racists in the South.

d. all of the above.

____ 7. Mickey Schwerner, James Chaney, and Andrew Goodman were

a. civil rights workers who were murdered during the summer of 1964.

b. the leaders of Freedom Summer.

c. the first three African Americans to register to vote during Freedom Summer.

d. three white men convicted of bombing an African American church in Mississippi.

____ 8. When Fannie Lou Hamer's boss warned her not to register to vote, Hamer

a. backed down to save her home and family.

b. ignored his threats and registered anyway.

c. told her husband to register for her.

d. warned other African Americans not to register.

____ 9. The Mississippi Freedom Democratic Party (MFDP)

a. challenged the whites-only regular Democratic party.

b. was organized to oppose the registration of African Americans.

c. was a political party that represented the views of the Ku Klux Klan.

d. was organized to make sure that no African Americans were elected to Congress.

III. Essay Write your answer to the following in paragraph form on a separate piece of paper.

10. The events of Freedom Summer had causes rooted in a system of injustice and discrimination. Many of the effects of that summer were long lasting. Discuss one cause and one effect of each of the following events: **a.** Three Civil Rights workers are found dead. **b.** Civil rights workers open Freedom Schools. **c.** The Mississippi Freedom Democratic Party goes to Atlantic City. **d.** Cities in the North are rocked by riots.

Case Study 7 Test: The Bitter Struggle of Malcolm X

Name: _____ Date: _____

I. Matching Decide which definition in the right column best explains a term in the left column. Then write the letter of that definition in the space next to the term.

____ 1. mosque

____ 2. nationalism

____ 3. symbol

____ 4. hustler

____ 5. recruit

a. a small-time crook

b. to get people to join a group or an organization

c. a word, picture, or thing that represents something else

d. a Muslim house of worship

e. devotion to a country or group

II. Multiple Choice Choose the answer that best completes the sentence or answers the question. Then write the letter of your choice in the space provided.

____ **6.** Marcus Garvey

a. believed that African Americans would only gain equality with whites through gaining pride in themselves.

b. and Martin Luther King, Jr., organized a march on Washington.

c. convinced Malcolm X to become a Muslim while he was in prison.

d. accompanied Malcolm X on his *hajj* to Mecca.

____ **7.** Elijah Muhammad was

a. arrested along with Malcolm Little during the 1940s.

b. head of the Nation of Islam.

c. recruited by Malcolm X to join the Nation of Islam.

d. one of the men arrested for the murder of Malcolm X.

____ **8.** Malcolm X felt that other African American civil rights leaders

a. were right in trying to achieve integration.

b. were better speakers than himself.

c. should not work with whites to win civil rights for African Americans.

d. were devoted to black nationalism.

____ **9.** Malcolm X's travels to the Middle East and Africa led him to the conclusion that

a. whites in the United States were influenced by a racist society.

b. African Americans should leave the United States.

c. all whites were indeed devils.

d. integration was the best way for African Americans to achieve equality.

III. Essay Write your answer to the following in paragraph form on a separate piece of paper.

10. After his trip to the Middle East and Africa, Malcolm X changed his views about white society in the United States. Compare and contrast Malcolm X's views before and after his trip. Address the following questions in your essay: What were Malcolm X's views before the trip? What events during the trip helped to change his mind? How did his ideas change once he returned to the United States?

Case Study 8 Test: Black Power!

Name: _____ **Date:** _____

I. Matching
Decide which definition in the right column best explains a term in the left column. Then write the letter of that definition in the space next to the term.

____ 1. exile

____ 2. Watts

____ 3. militant

____ 4. Black Power

____ 5. grassroots

a. ghetto in Los Angeles that was the site of a six-day riot in the summer of 1965

b. slogan used by followers of Stokely Carmichael who believed that the Civil Rights Movement needed a new direction

c. being forced to live in another country

d. to work at the local level

e. being aggressive and sometimes using force to fight for a cause

II. Multiple Choice
Choose the answer that best completes the sentence or answers the question. Then write the letter of your choice in the space provided.

____ 6. In 1962, James Meredith

a. was convicted for killing three civil rights workers in Mississippi.

b. became the first African American to enter the University of Mississippi.

c. became the first African American senator elected from the state of Alabama.

d. formed the Student Nonviolent Coordinating Committee (SNCC).

____ 7. The idea called Black Power

a. started right after the Civil War in the Deep South.

b. was that African Americans should rely on help from white society to gain equality.

c. incorporated the nonviolent idea of civil disobedience.

d. began in a speech made by Stokely Carmichael in 1966.

____ 8. The race riots of the mid-1960s started in the ghetto of

a. Watts.

b. Newark.

c. Detroit.

d. Chicago.

____ 9. The Kerner Commission

a. was an organization that studied voting patterns in Georgia.

b. was a group of business people who donated money to the Civil Rights Movement.

c. was organized to explore the source of the riots of the mid-1960s.

d. investigated the assassination of President Kennedy.

III. Essay
Write your answer to the following in paragraph form on a separate piece of paper.

10. How did the ideas of Martin Luther King, Jr., and Stokely Carmichael differ? What factors do you think account for the differences? Use facts from your reading to support your opinion.

Follow-Up Test: The Road Partly Traveled

Name: _____ **Date:** _____

I. Matching Decide which definition in the right column best explains a term in the left column. Then write the letter of that definition in the space next to the term.

_____ **1.** Kerner Commission

_____ **2.** assassin

_____ **3.** institution

_____ **4.** unemployed

_____ **5.** Voting Rights Act of 1965

a. a murderer, specifically someone who kills a public official

b. said that the United States was moving toward two separate and unequal societies—one black and one white

c. outlawed literacy tests as requirements to voter registration

d. a large organization such as a school, business, or hospital

e. not having a job

II. Multiple Choice Choose the answer that best completes the sentence or answers the question. Then write the letter of your choice in the space provided.

_____ **6.** By the late 1960s, Martin Luther King, Jr.,

a. believed that the key to ending violence was to wipe out poverty.

b. felt that the goals of the Civil Rights Movement had been achieved.

c. had become separated from the Civil Rights Movement he had helped found.

d. felt that segregation was the best way for the African American community to grow.

_____ **7.** The Poor People's Campaign was

a. an organization founded to help the homeless buy homes.

b. a grassroots attempt by white racist groups in the South to raise money to fight the Civil Rights Movement.

c. Martin Luther King, Jr.'s, attempt to wipe out poverty in the United States.

d. a movement to get legal protection for homeless whites in the North.

_____ **8.** By the early 1970s, African American participation in the military

a. increased.

b. decreased.

c. stayed about the same.

d. None of the above.

_____ **9.** Because of the Civil Rights Movement, African Americans

a. are able to register and vote in the South.

b. attend integrated schools.

c. are no longer forced to eat in separate restaurants.

d. All of the above.

III. Essay Write your answer to the following in paragraph form on a separate piece of paper.

10. The Civil Rights Movement has helped to bring about great changes in U.S. society. Discuss and describe two changes brought about by the Civil Rights Movement. Explain how the movement brought about these changes and how the African American community benefited from them. Then describe problems faced by the African American community today. How might another civil rights movement help to solve these problems?